DATE DUE

Z

Selection of New Suppliers
by the Mobile Family

Selection of New Suppliers by the Mobile Family

James E. Bell, Jr.

Assistant Professor of Marketing
Southern Illinois University
DeKalb, Illinois

ERRATUM

Dr. Bell is at Northern Illinois University,
not Southern Illinois University.

Dedicated to

my father and mother

for helping

Preface

This monograph is concerned with one of the many implications of our nation's phenomenal population mobility. It seeks to provide retailers and researchers with a better understanding of the process by which newly arrived families rebuild shopping patterns upon completion of a long distance move.

The doctoral research which resulted in this monograph started as a result of the author's experience in the food distribution industry. On the association level, the author was employed by the National Association of Food Chains during the inception of the *Progressive Grocer* Cleveland Kroger study. One part of this study included an investigation of the impact of geographic mobility upon supermarkets serving particular market areas. On the retail level, the author was associated with his parents in the development of a new supermarket in an unfamiliar market area. During this unsuccessful venture the new outlet attracted as permanent customers a rather large number of community newcomers. At the same time, heavy promotional expenditures and price leadership were unable to change the established shopping patterns of a sufficient number of permanent residents.

Findings presented will hopefully aid practitioners in many areas in structuring programs for the mobile market segment. Vast sums are now spent to change existing shopping patterns. Perhaps more efficiency can be gained by directing promotions specifically toward the mobile market. Moreover, marketers operating in areas where mobility is a constant operating problem might profitably consider the managerial suggestions incorporated in this work.

The author sincerely appreciates the help provided by the Bureau of Business and Economic Research, Graduate School of Business Administration, Michigan State University. The author, however, assumes full responsibility for any mistakes.

Acknowledgments

Completion of this work presents an opportunity to express sincere appreciation for the academic guidance and financial support which made it possible.

Dr. Bernard J. La Londe, chairman of the committee guiding the research, made a substantial contribution to the final work. In delaying personal projects which had far greater immediate personal rewards, Dr. La Londe earned the sincere gratitude of the author. Certainly, the time and ideas Dr. La Londe gave so freely helped formulate aspirations far beyond this work. The contributions of Dr. La Londe are sincerely appreciated.

The other members of the research committee, Dr. E. Jerome McCarthy and Dr. Paul E. Smith each made substantial contributions. In particular, the review Dr. McCarthy provided of the first draft provided the basis for several needed improvements in the content and structure of the final report. Dr. Smith was very helpful in offering suggestions on which areas the research should cover in providing added guidance in conversations as the work progressed.

Initial guidance for the research was provided through a conversation with the late Dr. E. A. Brand, Coordinator of the Food Marketing Program at Michigan State University for many years. The warm relationship enjoyed with Dr. Brand over a number of years made the graduate education experience much more meaningful.

Financially the research undertaking was made possible through scholarships received from three food industry firms: The Campbell Sales Company, Philip Morris, Inc., and The Sperry & Hutchinson Company. A full scholarship was received from The Sperry & Hutchinson Company, while partial scholarships were received from Philip Morris, Inc., and The Campbell Sales Company. The research could not have been carried out without the aid received from the food industry.

Dr. Thomas A. Staudt, former Chairman of the Department of Marketing and Transportation Administration, provided an opportunity to gain valuable teaching experience while enrolled in graduate school. The aid and guidance of Dr. Staudt over a period of years are sincerely appreciated.

In a very large part, numerous contacts with fellow graduate students aided the completion of the work. Acknowledgment of the help received is made to express sincere appreciation for many productive conversations.

Table of Contents

List of Tables

List of Figures

I

Problem Delineation

Each year approximately 20 percent of the nation's population moves. According to the Census figures, two-thirds of these movers stay within the same county, one-sixth go to a different county of the same state, and one-sixth move to another state.[1]

Bureau of Census projections for 1975 anticipate some 47 million people will make a change in residence that year. The estimate is based on a projected population of 226 million for the nation and a mobility rate of 20.8 percent a year by 1975.[2] Based on the classification of movers for March, 1965 to March, 1966, in 1975 some 15.6 million persons are expected to make long distance moves taking them outside the county in which they resided at the beginning of the year.

The geographically mobile segment of the population is now larger than the entire Negro population. Using the national mobility rate for 1948 to 1966 as a basis, all the occupants of the households in an average area would be expected to move within a five year period.

Nature and Background of the Problem

A change of residence creates a number of problems for the mobile family—the mobiles of the present study.

One of the problems is the selection of suppliers of goods and services in the area of the new residence.

The primary objective of this research is to investigate the economic decision process by which these geographically mobile consumers select new sources of supply for selected goods and services after completing a long distance move.

One study identifies the following socio-economic changes as the primary causes of the increased mobility of the United States population:

- Geographic mobility has accounted for the rural to urban migration, the growth of the suburbs, and in some cases the move back to the center city.

- New industries, business mergers, and transfers have resulted in the development of a group of affluent, mobile Americans who expect to move every few years.

- The impact of the migration of the Negro to the North, the growing concern for civil rights, and urban renewal programs have created another group of mobile people.

- Increases in military and governmental personnel have also added to the impact of geographic mobility upon the economy.[3]

In a ten-year period, 1954 to 1964, the Bureau of Census found only one out of every four people stayed in the same residence.[4]

Scope of the Problem

If a change in residence does not involve a long distance move the mobiles may retain many of the same sources of supply used before they moved. When the housewife is able to return to former suppliers the problems of adjusting to a new neighborhood may be eased. However, in long distance moves the distance involved may make the cost of returning to former suppliers prohibitive. In such cases movers are faced with the problem of selecting new suppliers.

After completing a long distance move, new sources of supply of goods and services must be sought; old shopping habits must be replaced.

Selection of new suppliers is a learning process, augmented by the family's previous experience. In selecting sources of supply from a number of competitors, consumers have to evaluate the merits of potential sources in terms of family needs, wants, and limitations.

New arrivals in a community must select suppliers in two distinct categories: goods and services. In selecting suppliers for specific types of goods, the presence of familiar chain outlets and recognizable brands of merchandise may ease the selection process. However, if newcomers find the chain outlet in the new community is substantially different from the store patronized in the prior community, store loyalty cannot be transferred. Whether a chain outlet eases the store selection problem for the newcomer depends on its similarity to the outlet in the old community.

If the mobile consumer has specific brand preferences, suppliers may be selected on that basis. However, where similar items have widespread distribution, the decision to select a particular supplier may turn on other factors such as convenience, price, credit or service.

In selecting suppliers for goods, information is easily available. However, in selecting suppliers for services, the process is somewhat more complicated. Perhaps the most difficult decision area is that of professional services, where advertising is prohibited by professional ethics. In the nonprofessional service area, the mobile family is faced with the problem of judging the credibility of the various information cues available. Such judgments are of particular importance where a service is purchased in conjunction with a product representing a major expenditure. Home remodeling is one example. However, in purchase categories where the service is relatively homogeneous, the decision to patronize a particular outlet may be made primarily on the basis of convenience.

A micro-economic analysis of economic decision making by mobile consumers will be the focal point of the research of the present study.

Statement of the Problem

The research investigates the decision process by which family suppliers are chosen from competing institutions, analyzes the decision-making process used in selecting suppliers for particular goods and services, and studies various information sources used by mobile consumers. Another area of the study investigates the division of decision responsibility within the family. Attention is also concentrated on how long mobiles take after arriving in a community to select suppliers in the categories under study, as well as how many suppliers are visited before one supplier is selected.

Specifically, the research is focused on the following questions about mobile consumers:

1. What types of decisions do they have to make?
2. Which member of the family selects the suppliers?
3. What sources of information are used?
4. How long after arriving in a community does it take before selections are made?
5. How many potential suppliers are visited before the selections are made?
6. What is the impact of socio-economic factors and family life cycle upon the process by which shopping patterns are rebuilt?

Hypotheses

The fundamental premise of this research is that socio-economic and life cycle characteristics of mobile families influence the decision-making process by which suppliers are chosen for selected goods and services. The research hypotheses are based on the premise that the dimensions of the decision processes of mobile families can be identified and analyzed. The research hypotheses cover five general areas of investigation:

1. The combined supplier selection patterns of the mobile consumers under study do not vary between purchase categories.[5]

2. Life cycle variables do not significally influence the division of decision-making responsibility within the family.
   A. The length of time a couple has been married does not significantly influence the division of decision-making responsibility for choosing family suppliers.
   B. Wives with one or more pre-school age children, five years old and less, do not have significantly less responsibility for selecting suppliers than do wives in all other families.

3. Income and occupation do not significantly influence the division of decision-making responsibility within the family.
   A. Income is not a significant factor in the division of decision responsibility within a mobile family.
   B. The occupation of the head of a mobile family is not a significant factor in determining the division of decision-making responsibility within the family.

4. The mobile consumers as a group do not identify one information source which is used significantly more than others in each of the supplier categories being investigated.
   A. There is not a significant relationship between the education of the head of a mobile family and the use of particular information sources in selecting suppliers.
   B. There is not a significant relationship between the education of a mobile housewife and the use of particular information sources in selecting suppliers.

C. The occupation of the head of a mobile family is not a significant factor in determining the information sources used in selecting suppliers for family needs.

D. The income of a mobile family is not a significant factor in determining the information source used in selecting suppliers.

E. Whether a family resides in a one-family or a multi-family dwelling is not a significant factor in determining the information source used in selecting suppliers.

5. There is not a significant relationship between a family's education, or the number of moves a family has made in the past decade, and the time taken to select new suppliers upon completion of a long distance move.

A. There is not a significant relationship between the educational level of the household head and the weeks taken to select favorite suppliers after completing a long distance move.

B. There is not a significant relationship between the educational level of the housewife and the weeks taken to select favorite suppliers after completing a long distance move.

C. There is not a significant relationship between the number of long distance moves a family has made in the past decade and the weeks taken to select favorite suppliers after completing a long distance move.

The study is based upon personal interviews with 147 long distance mobiles, all of whom had completed long distance moves into the metropolitan area studied.

A local welcoming organization provided the list of names from which the sample was drawn. Interviews were confined to families moving into the study area during the period April, 1966 through July, 1966. All families were asked by a telephone interviewer to participate in the study. The home interviews were made by women hired and trained for the research. The average interview took forty-five minutes to complete. All interviews were made with the housewife in each mobile family.

Upon completion of the interviews, which took place from ten to thirty weeks after the newcomers arrived in the community, data collected were transferred to punch cards and tabulated. Survey findings were subjected to statistical tests to prove or reject the research hypotheses.

Contributions of the Study

The primary contribution of the research is the development of a specific body of knowledge on the decision processes of a large, unique, and identifiable segment of the consumer market. This knowledge can be used by manufacturers and retailers in adjusting market offerings to consumer needs.

Marketing involves a flow of goods and services accompanied by a parallel flow of information between buyers and sellers. Through increased knowledge of mobile shopping patterns, the productivity of both parties in market transactions may be increased. This research will provide potentially valuable information to firms attempting to focus upon the mobile market.

Consumer behavior research has in the past been primarily concerned with the decision processes by which families decide to purchase one specific item or another, or one brand rather than another. This work contributes to the existing knowledge by analyzing the decision process by which families select suppliers. The research is also directed at determining if significant differences exist in the decision processes of families possessing differing socio-economic and life cycle characteristics.

Three previous studies have particular relevance to this research. The first, based upon 148 long distance geographically mobile families, found the market segment to be easily identifiable and representative of a quality market when compared with the rest of the population. The research found the segment has a higher level of education, income, and occupational status than the rest of the population. Willingness to be mobile, high aspirations, and youth were also found to be distinguishing characteristics of the market.[6]

The second study in the area revealed that the proportion of mobile consumers making purchases of durable goods in a given year was close to 50 percent greater than the proportion of nonmovers.[7] A third study stressed that while mobiles have habits just as nonmovers do, mobiles are psychologically as well as physically more predisposed to changes in environment.[8]

Market segmentation as a concept separates identifiable consumer groups with a view to improving marketing efficiency. This research on a portion of the consumer market, comprising nearly 13 million people, is an attempt to improve marketing productivity and effectiveness through a deeper understanding of consumer behavior. The findings are important to both manufacturers and retailers.

To the manufacturer, the work in areas of communications and distribution offers valuable information on the learning process by which mobile consumers acquire new suppliers. By evaluating the findings, manufacturers may better decide whether market coverage is adequate to withstand the impact of mobility upon family loyalty to brand and to product.

To retailers operating from a limited number of fixed locations, the research offers a better insight into the ferment taking place in separate market areas as families move. This ferment is a constant problem to suppliers operating within particularly mobile market areas, but at the same time makes possible an adjustment in merchandising policies. To manufacturers, population mobility may only mean familiar products are being purchased from different outlets. To the retailer, a change in residence may mean the loss of regular customers and necessitate a program designed to capture replacements.

Limitations of the Study

The limitations of the research are as follows:

1. The study was confined geographically to one metropolitan area. Only families moving into the area during four consecutive months, April through July, 1966, were included in the sample.

2. All families included in the sample were obtained from a list maintained by a local welcoming organization. In gathering names of newcomers the organization used several different sources, primarily, public utilities. The survey is limited by the completeness of the lists maintained by the cooperating organization.

3. To be included in the research a family had to complete a long distance move into the metropolitan area under study from outside the three-county area of the community. In addition, the principal county in which the research was conducted has three principal employers: a major university, the major sales and manufacturing facility of an automobile producer, and numerous offices associated with a major governmental unit. All university students were excluded from the sample. The families interviewed reflected the dominant positions of the three major employers in the area.

4. The research was conducted by interviewing only the housewives in the families and the answers received were dependent upon their recall ability. The research should be evaluated in light of the fact that only one visit was made to each household and the sample did not include a cross section of the entire population.

II

The Mobile Consumer
and Marketing Decisions

The Concept of Market Segmentation

Since World War II, customer- and market-oriented firms have stressed the renewal of the premise that businesses should operate to benefit consumers as well as businessmen. The premise, generally referred to as the marketing concept, is founded on the principle that business firms should plan and organize business strategies based on a careful review of the needs, forces, and opportunities in the markets. Fred J. Borch stressed that under the marketing concept the consumer becomes the fulcrum about which the business operates for the balanced best interests of all concerned.[1]

The renewal of the marketing concept is based, according to J. U. McNeal, upon an understanding of consumer behavior.[2] Implementation of the concept is dependent upon a translation, by businessmen, of market knowledge into effective corporate strategies. In describing the managerial functions of marketing, Thomas A. Staudt stressed that market delineation, "the determination of potential purchasers and their identifying characteristics," is the first prerequisite for effective marketing performance.[3]

10

A major area of development on consumer behavior has been concerned with attempts at segmentating the consumer market into various categories or sub-markets. The use of segmentation has facilitated the development of marketing strategies aimed at relatively distinguishable and sometimes homogeneous groups of consumers.[4]

In one of the more valuable works on segmentation, Wendall R. Smith stated that the demand side of the market segmentation represents a rational adjustment of product and marketing effort to consumer or user requirements. In the language of the economist, segmentation is a disaggregative process aimed at developing several demand schedules where only one was recognized before.[5] Emphasis upon market segmentation may be viewed as a condition or cost of growth. Smith found that once the core markets have been developed the process turns to keying efforts to distinguish market areas for special products and marketing effort.

Utilizing the concept of market segmentation, characteristics of markets have been identified based upon such concepts as race,[6] sex,[7] age,[8, 9] income,[10] geographic location,[11] and occupation.[12]

Other research in the area of market segmentation has dealt with the identification of less distinguishable features such as social class,[13] personality type,[14, 15] and innovativeness.[16] In particular, the work of James M. Carman on the application of social class to market segmentation found that it is possible to subdivide classes into gross but homogeneous groups which can be easily identified. The findings of the research were, however, insufficient as to the practicality in planning marketing strategies for each sub-class or segment.[17]

The Mobile Market Segment

One particularly large and distinguishable segment of the consumer market is composed of the individuals in the geographically mobile segment of the population. The proportion of the nation's population in this mobile market segment, according to the annual surveys conducted since 1948, has ranged from 18.6 to 21.0 percent.[18] From March, 1965 to March, 1966 the mobility rate was 19.3 percent or 36.7 million people. Of the 36.7 million people changing addresses in the March, 1965-66 period, 24.2 million moved within counties and the remaining 12.5 million moved to a different county. The intercounty movers were divided equally between those moving within a state and those moving between states or from abroad.[19]

The 12.5 million people who moved to a different county during the March, 1965 to March, 1966 period consisted of two groups of nearly equal size:

- Group A: the 3.3 percent of the nation's population which moved to a different county within the same state or the intrastate migrants.
- Group B: the 3.3 percent of the nation's population which moved to a new residence from a different state or from abroad.[20]

Based upon information obtained from population mobility surveys for 1964, 1965, and 1966, the following data summarize the relationship between selected population characteristics and the distance moved:

Sex-difference. The mobility of males was slightly greater than that of females in all classifications: intracounty moves, intrastate moves, and interstate moves.

Age. Young adults, 18 to 34 years old, had a higher mobility rate than all other age groups. The proportion of young adult movers who were migrants, or intercounty movers, was greater than the corresponding proportion for either persons 35 years old and over or for those under 18.

Color. The non-white population had a higher mobility rate (24 percent) than the white population (19 percent). The excess was largely due to local mobility. Approximately 33 percent of the white intercounty moves and nearly 40 percent of the non-white intercounty moves were to a different state.

Education. Persons who had completed one or more years of college were found to be somewhat more mobile than individuals who had completed less than one year.

Employment status. Unemployed men had a higher total mobility rate (30 percent) than employed men (20 percent). Nearly 41 percent of the mobile unemployed were migrants, whereas the comparable figure for the mobile employed was 32 percent.

Professional workers. The mobility rate of professional workers was 3 percent above that of the other non-agriculture workers. Mobile professional workers were more likely to have completed a move into a different county (46 percent) than other mobile workers (29 percent).[21]

The relatively high proportion of migrants among whites, persons completing one or more years of college, and professional workers, suggests a positive relationship between socio-economic status and migration. At the same time the relatively high proportion of migrants among unemployed men suggests a negative relationship. Thus migrants appear to be of two kinds: the unemployed who move to search for job opportunities elsewhere, and those holding professional positions who move in response to a greater demand for services elsewhere. The migration from the rural south to the urban north of the relatively poor and uneducated to states several hundred miles away is a clue to the possible negative relationship between socio-economic status and migration.[22]

Another study revealed that about 65 percent of the migrants cited job-related circumstances as reasons for moving. The remaining 35 percent gave housing, 10 percent; changes in family status, 11 percent; and other reasons, 14 percent. Among the major reasons related to work were "to take a job," "to look for work" and "job transfer." The study suggests that migration occurs primarily in response to circumstances relating to employment, whereas local mobility is more closely related to housing arrangements.[23]

A study of 148 long distance mobiles conducted in Philadelphia during 1964 was concerned with determining if the long distance mobile group is significantly superior or inferior according to four criteria: level of spending power, potential for future increased spending power, present purchase behavior, and potential for change in future purchase behavior. The results of the study revealed that geographic mobiles possess the following characteristics as a particular market segment:

- Relatively young (and in the early stages of the family life cycle)
- Well educated
- In higher status occupations
- Having above average incomes
- In higher social classes
- Socially active
- Socially upward mobile, with high social class aspirations
- Geographically mobile in the past
- Having their present move economically inspired.[24]

The value to marketers of segmenting the entire mobile market for specific programs depends upon the degree to which a change in residence may affect a change in purchase patterns. To the nearly 13 percent of the nation's population which moves each year within a relatively small local radius, changes in purchase patterns are rather limited. However, in terms of the 13 million long distance mobiles, where a change in address presents critical problems associated with adjusting to a new environment, the marketing opportunities appear to be substantial. Long distance mobiles are an important target for two prime reasons:

(1) Mobiles are a market for firms associated with the uprooting, moving, and settling of mobile individuals.

(2) Mobiles, once the move has been completed, represent a potential market for all suppliers in the area of the new residence.

Key Components of the Consumer Decision Process

Information Sources

The need of newcomers for information on products and supplies is not a problem solely pertaining to mobiles. One author wrote that it is universally acknowledged that consumers lack knowledge to some degree and stressed that no systematic effort has been made to probe the size of the deficiency.[25]

Another research study found that two broad types of information are used by new families in a community in selecting medical doctors. *Non personal* sources of information, such as the yellow pages, or the local medical society, were used when the person making the selection decision was over thirty-five years of age, on the upper level of the socio-economic spectrum, did not have children, and selected a physician in the first month in the new community. *Personal professional sources* were used when the decision maker was over thirty-five years of age, at the upper end of the socio-economic spectrum, had a greater than average number of children, and did not select a doctor during the first two months in a new residence.[26]

The research of Feldman and Spencer also found that when decision makers sought information from a personal, nonprofessional source, 60 percent of the time they selected people without professional background—friends, neighbors, and co-workers, for example. The decision makers in this research were usually thirty-five years old or younger; they were in the middle of the socio-economic spectrum, and tended not to select a physician until the second or third month of residence. It was also found that people seeking medical advice often rely upon persons older than themselves.

Information sources, other than information obtained from searching, were also classified into personal sources and impersonal sources in research on new product adoption. It was found that all face-to-face information was judged highly credible since the receivers knew the people providing the information as friends and they were understood, believed, and willing to answer questions. Impersonal sources such as the mass media were viewed as less satisfactory sources of communication because of the unwillingness of people to attach a high degree of credibility to the sources.[27]

An important problem of information, the determination of market price, was discussed by George J. Stigler in terms of a phenomenon he called *search*. He viewed the search for information as a process by which the marginal cost (MC) of search is equated to the marginal revenue (MR) obtained from the search.

In an article on consumer information, Stigler identified the following three key variables as determining the degree of search to be initiated: (1) the larger the percent of the buyer's expenditures on the commodity, the greater the potential savings from the search, (2) the lower the fraction of repetitive (experienced) buyers in the market, the greater the amount of search, (3) the larger the cost of the search, the greater the size of the market.[28] Two important references to advertising were also made by Stigler. He stressed that advertising is, among other things, a method of providing potential buyers with knowledge of the identity of sellers. In this regard Stigler viewed advertising as an immensely powerful influence in the elimination of ignorance. He also viewed advertising as a decisive influence in the dispersion of price information making the searching process much more economical.

The sources of information used by southern housewives in food product buying decisions were reviewed in a report by John B. Roberts. The report dealing with the factors influencing food buying decisions presented data on the kinds of groups most likely to respond to different promotional efforts.[29]

Information influencing food buying decisions was found to come first from containers, cans, and labels; secondly, through requests from children and family members; third, newspaper and grocery advertisements; fourth, cookbooks and coupons.

Roberts also reported that as the age of the housewife increased, the influence exerted by such factors as boxes, cans, labels, and recipes declined. Responses to information received from children were particularly important to wives in the thirty to fifty age groups. Research also found that the influence of family, friends, and relatives increased consistently with higher levels of education. Furthermore, the homemakers whose income and education were above average responded to the widest variety of stimuli.

In research on the sources of information used by housewives, James H. Myers found that upper-class housewives had more opportunities to develop informal communication networks. These women more frequently had club memberships and participated in social meetings with friends, neighbors, and relatives. This social interaction brought them more information about new products. Housewives having less free time depended upon information received from the mass media. The level of informal communication networks was appreciably less than in the upper class families and consequently the total information received on new products was less than where the informal communications networks were well established.[30]

Reference groups are an important source of information for consumers on all levels of society. One author found that a group of friends, colleagues or neighbors usually has similar needs, attitudes and expectations, thus forming for each other a reference group.[31] Researchers also found in studying the purchases of large household appliances that more than one-half of the buyers turned to acquaintances for advice and in many cases looked at the appliances they used. The buyers typically bought a brand seen in the home of a friend or relative.[32]

In perhaps the most widely quoted study on reference groups, Elihu Katz and Paul F. Lazarsfeld found in the Decatur study that marketing leaders and taste leaders are present in almost equal numbers in high, middle, and low status groups.[33] Market leaders on all levels of society were found to exhibit the same general characteristics. However, their research found a concentration of leadership among the larger families on all levels of society. Leaders were also generally a bit older than the person asking advice and were likely "wives" and "gregarious."

In a study of reference groups, William H. Whyte, Jr., found that as consumers became more experienced more interest was expressed in the pros and cons of makes, models, sizes, and potential economies. Venders could not satisfy the curiosity. Advertising did not give as much product information as wanted, and gave very little believable comparative information.

So it is to the reference group that the consumer turns. It is not so much that the consumers are distrustful of what manufacturers say about products; the consumer is curious. Once, the retailer was the key factor in the marketing of new appliances. Today, if the customer has not already sold himself or been pre-sold by friends, the consumer is not likely to go into a store, because he feels little can be learned in the store. The real selling job is done before the customer makes contact with the dealer. Thanks to the social group's guidance the consumer has already determined almost everything about the product.[34]

Another author wrote that the degree to which man's behavior is influenced by other individuals, in the market place or out, varies depending upon the decision circumstances and the nature of the product.[35] He also stated that in the marketing process determinants vary primarily according to the matter to be decided, such as the attributes or product in the market place. The research showed that the degree to which a product is apparent is an important factor in determining the susceptibility of the product to reference group influence.

Decision Making

Upon moving to a new community families must go about the process of acquiring sources of supply for all the goods and services they need. Shopping habits which were broken through a move must be rebuilt or re-established through a learning process. Decisions must not only be made on whether to buy or not to buy an item, but also on the source of supply for each item. Responsibility for the decision must be assigned within the family unit.

In an article on buying behavior, Frederick E. May explained buying decisions as a learning process, with different amounts of exploratory search effort depending on various conditions that take place where uncertainty exists about product quality.[36] He found that the effort or deliberation was dependent upon income, amount of purchase as a percent of income, education level, availability of special opportunity to purchase, urgency of product need, and whether experience with product or supplier was satisfactory before.

In an extensive bibliography on consumer behavior, James Morgan described the work done by George Katona and Eva Mueller as the most extensive study on information getting, shopping, and decision making within the family. A number of indexes on various aspects of decision making and information getting were combined into one over-all index of deliberation in an attempt to see why some persons are more deliberate and circumspect than others.[37]

The work by Katona and Mueller showed great variation in the care with which consumer decisions were made from one purchase to another. However, data did show that consumers were much more deliberate with large, durable goods purchased than with non-durable goods. It was found that individual buyer characteristics and the conditions with which the purchase takes place had a bearing on the decision-making process. The most deliberate decision making tended to occur when the individual concerned had a college education, had an income of between $5,000 and $7,500, was under 35 years of age, and was a white collar worker who expressed a liking for shopping around.[38]

Deliberation appeared to be less extensive when the income of the buyer was relatively high or the price paid was relatively low; also when the education of the buyer was low. The authors emphasized that the variables alone do not explain all the findings. In general, they concluded that under conditions of alternatives and consequences, discussion with family members and extensive information seeking tend to occur when buyers have the discretion to act, and when it matters greatly how they act.

The study by Katona and Miller also found that as the size of the expenditure increases, particularly in furniture, decisions tend to be jointly made—although the husband dominates in the automobile field.

In the Sharp and Mott study of decisions in the metropolitan family, findings indicated a great deal of joint decision making. At the same time an understood division of responsibility tended to grow more pronounced with increasing age and length of marriage.[39] Regarding expressed buying plans, the study found husbands and wives show a very similar frequency in planning expenditures. The differences that do appear between husbands' and wives' plans suggest that wives' plans are slightly better thought out. While wives are less confident of fulfilling the plans mentioned, they experience a higher rate of fulfillment throughout all areas studies. The finding may have been attributable to the role of wives in handling the budget and thus being in a better position to judge realistically, according to Sharp and Mott.

The authors also reported that in consumer surveys concerned with a broad range of expenditures, husbands and wives are equally desirable respondents. However, if reactions are sought to specific features of an automobile, for example, husbands might be better respondents. Conversely, wives might be preferred for a detailed study of household goods.

A laboratory study of decision making by William F. Kenkel dealt with the process by which fifty married college couples decided how to spend $300 in a one-hour laboratory situation. The stipulation of the research was that each couple had to make decisions on how to spend the money on items they had not previously decided to buy. The research study measured the amount of total talking done by each partner, whose ideas were accepted or rejected, and any social or emotional actions.[40]

The findings pointed out that frequently husbands do more of the talking and contribute more ideas toward a solution of the problem. But in some cases, in the study by Kenkel, wives out-performed the husbands in talking and contributing ideas. In Kenkel's study the wives were observed to do more to keep the decision-making session running smoothly, but sometimes husbands played the role. Couples varied, too, with regard to which spouse was most influential.

Feldman and Spencer, in research on selecting medical services, reported that decisions rested in the hands of the wife 74 percent of the time, with the husband 11 percent of the time, and were made jointly only 15 percent of the time. The probability of a joint decision was greater if: (1) the wife was not employed outside the home, (2) the duration of marriage was greater than five years, (3) the age difference between the husband and wife was less than two years, (4) the selection of a doctor was made during the first month in a new community (5) the source of information was someone who shared a social (non-medical) relationship with the decision maker.[41]

One author, writing on the "Interacting Roles of the Household Purchasing Agent," developed an interesting thesis on the present role of the wife as the household purchasing agent. He pointed out that careful observations have shown that the housewife has an ever-increasing area of responsibility as the household purchasing agent. As the urban industrial society has developed, research evidence suggests the economic role of the husband has become more precisely and narrowly defined. At the same time the role of the wife as the steward of the family purse has been openly recognized.[42]

The wife was found by Whiteside to have responsibility for all food and clothing, except some men's articles, while the husband was to some degree a participant in decisions on shelter and furniture. Health expenditures were largely the responsibility of the wife. Educational expenditures were joint affairs. The annual vacation was even found to be a joint selection. Only in two major areas, automobiles and insurance, was the involvement of the housewife minimal.

In detailing a model on customer decision making, one author suggested that a model offers the best way to organize a framework and analyze the central element in the marketing system. The model offered several questions pertaining to the relationship between individual characteristics and the uses of information sources used in the process of shopping.[43]

Shopping Behavior

The process by which consumers select suppliers for their needs is conditioned by the socio-economic characteristics of the consumers, the suppliers available to them, and by the ease with which they can view the offerings of competing suppliers. A study of consumer shopping behavior focusing upon the family unit must attempt to describe the reasons for one or more acts of choice, either at a given time or over a period of time.

The *Chicago Tribune* studies revealed a close relationship between choice of store, patterns of spending, and class membership. People were found to be very realistic in the way personal value and expectations were matched with the status of a particular store. Department stores were found to have a definite social status in the eyes of the women shoppers. The social status became the primary basis of definition for the shopper. The research findings of the Tribune indicated that the most important function of retail advertising today, when prices and quality have become so standard, is to permit the shopper to make social class identification.[44]

The Tribune research found: (1) There is a social class system operative in metropolitan markets that can be isolated and described. (2) It is important to realize there are far-reaching psychological differences between the classes. (3) Consumption patterns operate as prestige symbols to define class membership, which is a more significant means of determining economic behavior than more income.

In research on the types and sources of information consumers used in purchasing living room furniture and television sets two authors defined shopping as a process of looking for information. Such information hopefully enabled the potential buyer to make satisfactory purchasing decisions. The process is aimed, as described by these authors, at the purchase of a product that will fulfill the needs, desires, and financial circumstances of the purchasing unit.[45]

The research also was aimed at establishing the relative importance of out-of-store information, newspapers, and talking with friends, as compared with the value of information obtained from visits to stores. Respondents recalled using information received in store visits in 41.4 percent of the purchases, information from friends in 29.7 percent of the purchases, and information from newspapers in 26.4 percent of the purchases. The heavy role played by information within retail stores was thought to be the result of the importance consumers placed on data concerning quality and service. Another interesting point revealed in the research was that purchasers do not shop extensively from store to store. The average furniture purchaser visited 3.3 stores while the average TV purchaser visited 2.2 stores before buying.

In selecting suppliers from which to make a purchase the cost of the item is not the only cost to be considered by the family. The cost of an item to a consumer, according to Wesley C. Bender, is a composite cost of the commodity, plus the costs incurred in achieving possession of the goods or service. The secondary purchase costs included: price costs—parking fees, installation fees, and credit charges; time costs—walking time, travel time, and searching time; and psychological costs—frustrating conflict and store layout anxiety.[46]

Bender further stated that consumers, not being rational, may not consider all costs. Yet since they are not totally naive, they will consider many of the costs.

Store patronage motives were divided into three major categories by Louis P. Bucklin.

(1) *Convenience Stores*—these stores for which the consumer has a preference before a need for some product arises. Usually the most accessible store.

(2) *Shopping Stores*—here the consumer has not developed a complete preference map relative to the products he wishes to buy. In such cases, the consumer must construct such a map before purchase.

(3) *Specialty Stores*—these are the stores in which the consumer has a willingness to shop even though it may not be the most accessible. When a need arises the consumer is willing to exert the special effort to reach the store.[47]

Such a classification is aimed at segmentation of the retail market so that the marketing strategies of retailers may be better directed. It also provides a method of classifying buying motives on something besides the products involved.

An experiment was reported in the *Journal of Marketing Research* by Richard N. Cardozo on a classroom laboratory study of shopping effort in which students were asked to take data from catalogs. The experiment showed that under certain conditions, efforts and expectation affected the evaluation of the product and of the experience. When expectations were unrealized, subjects rated both the product and shopping experience unfavorable. Expenditures of high effort moderated the effect, and for the shopping experience partially modified it.[48]

The author emphasized the limitations of the research, but had found that people at times use expectations as guidelines for evaluation. Thus, if a product does not measure up to expectations and the purchaser spent little effort, the outcome will really hurt sales. However, if the consumer spent a great deal of effort and the product is equal to the one in which little purchase effort was extended, it is not likely to hurt sales.

Another researcher wrote that while consumers have mobility in shopping it comes at the cost of time, effort, and money. Resistance exists to going further or expending more effort than necessary for the goods needed. Typically, consumers will buy at the nearest store, unless advantages of product quality, product selection, price or service lead them to go further. The truism is the premise underlying the development of the retail structure.[49]

The danger of asking people why they shop at certain stores was pointed out in another study. The study reported that attitudinal surveys can be misleading in that they may confuse attitudes which predispose patronage with those resulting from patronage. A possible answer might be to cross-tabulate consumer ranking of competing stores with data on the relative size of the expenditure in each store.[50]

The inherent danger of patronage studies was felt by the author to be so great that he felt it is desirable, perhaps essential, to secure the places and volume of patronage. The challenge is to find some means of distinguishing between attitudes which predispose persons toward patronage of given stores and those which result from patronage.

In the book, *What Makes Women Buy*, Janet Wolff says that convenience and loyalty play the major part in the choosing of stores by women. However, women remain loyal or pick one place of equal convenience over another partially due to mental characteristics. Women tend to personalize selections and identify themselves with many things about them. They tend to fit stores closely into their own personalities and lives.[51]

In research on the images of supermarkets in the minds of college student couples Kenward L. Atkin found that predisposition arising from prior store patronage is a powerful influence in store selection. Married couples who shopped at a store of a chain before moving tended to shop at outlets of the chain following the move. The search also found that families visit two or three food stores within their first week or two after establishing residence in the new community.[52]

The Progressive Grocer Study in the Cleveland area dealt in part with the selection of supermarkets by mobile families. Major findings of the study reveal that: (1) newcomers to a neighborhood make the first visit to a local store primarily because of convenience; (2) 65 percent of the families visit four or less supermarkets before picking a favorite, and (3) the favorite store is picked out three to six weeks after arriving in a community.[53]

The research also pointed up that 74 percent of the families moving to a new home were not asked by a local supermarket for business. In cases where the newcomers were contacted, the patronage results seemed to indicate a very favorable result for the program.[54]

Summary

Renewed interest in consumer-oriented marketing programs in the past twenty years has led to frequent attempts at market segmentation. The process of segmentation is aimed at determining differences among buyers so that marketing programs may be focused upon identified portions of the total consumer market.

The most frequently used segmentation variables have been socio-economoic in nature: (1) occupation, (2) income, (3) education, (4) sex, and (5) age. Additional segmentation has been done based upon family life cycle and geography. Segmentation is, in effect, an attempt to adjust product and marketing effort to consumer or user requirements.

The process of segmentation is aimed first at the identification of distinguishable features and secondly at determining the practicality of planning marketing strategies for the subgroup or segment. One easily identifiable and distinguishable segment of the consumer market is comprised of people in the geographically mobile segment of the population. Over 36 million people are in the mobile market segment which is composed of intracounty or local movers and intercounty or long distance movers. The segment of the mobile market, comprised of the nearly thirteen million long distance mobiles presents a group that is not only identifiable, but relatively homogeneous for the development of marketing programs. In particular, long distance mobile family units represent a market opportunity for firms associated with the uprooting, moving and settling of mobile individuals. Secondly, newcomers are a potential market for firms or individuals marketing goods and services in the area of the new residence.

In the process of adjusting to a new community, mobiles are faced with the problem of rebuilding their sources of supply. In the rebuilding process, concern turns first to gathering information on available suppliers, second to determining the division of decision responsibility for selecting suppliers within the family, and third, with undertaking the shopping process by which suppliers are selected.

Research on the consumer market has shown three general classes of available information: personal, impersonal, and searching. Personal information is generally viewed as highly credible in nature. Impersonal information (mass media, for example) is generally viewed with some reservation. Reference groups are a highly influential source of information. The larger expenditures in particular have been found to be highly influenced by reference groups.

In the area of decision responsibility, research has been concentrated upon the assignment of decision responsibility for selecting various goods or services within the family. Little research has been reported on which family member selects sources of supply for various goods or services.

The decision-making process within the family unit is a learning process involving various degrees of searching effort in an attempt to resolve uncertainty. Indexes on family decision making have shown great variations in the amount of care consumers have exhibited in selecting a product or service. Consumers have been shown to make decisions more deliberately on products which are durable and represent rather large expenditures. In research on family decision making, husbands and wives have been found to be equally desirable respondents to survey questions. Increased urbanization of the nation's population has tended to place more of the decisions on family purchases in the hands of the housewife. In particular, evidence points up that joint family decisions diminish as families have increased years of marriage. After a number of years of marriage, a division of decision responsibility tends to become apparent in each family.

Studies on shopping behavior have shown that people realistically match personal value and expectations with the status of a particular store. It was found that retail advertising serves consumers in part through providing the social class identification of the store. Shopping visits to a store are a prime means of providing information on products purchased. Item cost is not the only cost a customer incurs in making a purchase. Such additional shopping costs as parking fees, travel time, searching time, and psychological costs must also be evaluated.

Laboratory studies on shopping have shown that expectations and effort affect the evaluation of the product or of the service purchased. An extended effort to acquire a product will usually result in a favorable evaluation of it. However, in instances where it is relatively easy to acquire a product or service, if the purchased item or service is somewhat less than expected, a poor rating will frequently be given the purchased goods or service. Consumer behavior research has shown that a real danger lies in asking people why they patronize specific stores. A possible solution to the problem has been to cross tabulate consumer rankings of patronage and attitude. The possible bias in strictly attitude surveys is then minimized through including the actual purchase data pertaining to each family.

Additional studies on convenience and patronage have shown that store familiarity is a key element in the selection of new suppliers. Families shopping with a particular chain before moving tend to shop with the chain after moving.

III

Research Design

The research design of this study was confined to an investigation of the process by which families, possessing specific characteristics, chose selected suppliers upon completion of a long distance move. Characteristics which the families possessed were identified as independent variables. The factors which affect the selection process were identified as conditioning variables. Supplier categories studied were identified as dependent variables. A detailed description of the variables is contained in Figures 1, 2, and 3.

Independent Variables

Selected characteristics of mobile families were identified as independent variables. The socio-economic characteristics were: education of the household head and spouse, income of the family, occupation of the household head, and the number of families residing in the dwelling. The life cycle characteristics were the number of years of marriage and the age of the children (see Figure 1).

Dependent Variables

Suppliers selected by families in the categories under study in this research were identified as dependent variables. Selections were based upon the following rationale:

FIGURE 1
A Model of Selected Elements of Decision Making by Long Distance Movers

Family Characteristics	*Conditioning Elements*	*Supply Categories Selected for Patronage*
Independent Variables	*Conditioning Variables*	*Dependent Variables*

Independent Variables

SOCIO-ECONOMIC VARIABLES
Education of household head and spouse

Family income

Occupation of household head

Number families in dwelling

LIFE-CYCLE VARIABLES
Number years of marriage

Age of children

Conditioning Variables

Purchase Environment
Type of good or service needed

Distance from suppliers

Decision Responsibility
Household head or spouse

Joint decision

Family Experiences
Store loyalty

Brand familiarity

Number of long distance moves made since 1956

Sources of Information Used in Purchases
Personal sources

Impersonal sources

Searching process

Dependent Variables

GOODS
Food
Appliances
Furniture

CLOTHING
Men's suits
Women's best dresses

SERVICES

PERSONAL
Dry cleaners
Beauty shop
Financial institutions
Insurance
  1) Property
  2) Life
  3) Automobile

PROFESSIONAL
Doctor
  1) Family—G.P.
  2) Specialist
Dentist

FIGURE 2
Selected Supply Areas Chosen for Analysis
(Dependent Variables)

Searching Effort	*Goods*	*Services*	*Frequency of Use*
Minimum	Food	Dry cleaners Beauty shop	Most

Moderate	Appliances
	Furniture
		Financial
		Institutions
		  Banks
		  Credit unions
		  Savings/Loan
		Insurance
		  Property
		  Life
		  Automobile	

Extensive	Clothing
	  Men's suit's
	  Women's best
	    dresses
		Doctor
		  General
		    practitioner
		  Specialist
		Dentist
			Least

FIGURE 3
Outline of the Research Thrust

Independent Variables		*Conditioning Variables*	*Dependent Variables*		
Mobile families possessing specific socio-economic and life cycle characteristics	*and*	conditioned by prior experience and supplier selection patterns	*after a move*	select specific suppliers	for goods and services.

1. They were common household items representing an array of goods and services normally purchased by families.

2. They represented varying purchase problems encountered by consumers in selecting sources of supply.

3. They were classified by the degree of searching effort consumers were likely to spend in selecting suppliers in particular areas of expenditure and by the frequency with which suppliers were used.

4. They represented a dollar expenditure that was significant enough for families to be able to recall their purchase decisions (see Figure 2).

Methodology

Research findings were developed from a detailed study of 147 new families in a metropolitan area of 200,000. A local welcoming organization provided the study universe: families subscribing to various utilities, applying for drivers licenses, and requesting new charge accounts. All families interviewed arrived in the community between April 1 and July 31, 1966. Arrivals from a two-quarter period were used to minimize possible bias which might result from seasonal moving patterns.

Sixty percent of the families interviewed had moved to the study area from another state. Women interviewers held comprehensive in-the-home interviews with housewives of families who had been in the community a mean time of twenty-three weeks. A 20 percent call-back was made to confirm all interview information.

While the rationale developed was not expected to apply to all family decisions, it did provide a logical framework for the categorization of the purchase areas studied in the research. A detailed description of the purchase categories investigated includes the following:

Food: all food and non-foods purchased from supermarkets and other food stores to be used within the house.

Beauty parlors: all services dealing with the hair of the housewife.

Dry cleaning: all services dealing with the dry cleaning of family garments, both conventional and self-service.

Financial institutions: all financial services received from banks, saving and loan firms and credit unions.

Insurance: all insurance policies purchased and companies chosen in the automobile, property and life insurance areas.

Furniture: all purchases of furniture, draperies, and carpets of $25.00 or more.

Appliances: all purchases of major household appliances of $25.00 or more.

Women's clothing: women's dresses and suits for social occasions.

Men's suits: all men's suits, sport coat and dress/slack combinations.

Medical services: the general practitioner, specialist, and dentist providing medical attention to family members.

Conditioning Variables

The decision process by which a mobile family selected suppliers was thought to be affected by a number of interwoven factors operating between the stimuli of the market and the characteristics of the family. In this research, conditioning variables were identified as: the purchase environment, the division of decision responsibility within the family, past experiences of the family, and the sources of information used in making purchases (see Figure 1). The conditioning variables were identified as the mediating factors which provided the atmosphere in which the decision process took place (see Figure 3).

In addition to securing data necessary to test the hypotheses for each purchase category chosen, the research was also concerned with data on (1) credit, (2) brand and store loyalty, (3) trading stamps, (4) reasons for selecting particular suppliers, (5) the degree of transferred loyalty, and (6) dollar expenditures for furniture and appliances. Questions pertaining to the areas were incorporated in the final research design.

IV

Presentation of Findings

Combined Supplier Selection Pattern

The first hypothesis of this study was formulated to test the variation of supplier selection patterns in different purchase categories. The hypothesis states that the combined supplier selection patterns of mobiles do not vary from one purchase category to another.

Research in this study showed that the combined supplier selection patterns of the mobile consumers under study varied from one purchase category to another. Differences between the selection patterns were based upon the nature of the goods or services being acquired rather than upon the characteristics of the families making supplier selections.

The combined supplier selection pattern is composed of four elements: information sources used by families in selecting suppliers, the individuals making the purchase decision in each category, the time taken by mobile families to select new suppliers upon completion of a move, and the number of potential suppliers visited before a supplier is selected within a purchase category.

Information Sources Used

Mobiles used personal information more than any other source in rebuilding shopping patterns. Searching was the second most vital means of gaining potential supplier information. In no purchase category did newcomers place primary reliance on impersonal information sources. For example, almost no use was made of yellow-page advertisements. Furniture and appliance purchases were the only categories where newspapers played a vital role in shopper selections.

Each purchase category had one strongly preferred information source. Personal information provided the bulk of data in eight supplier categories: (1) beauty parlors, (2) dry cleaners, (3) financial institutions, (4) insurance, (5) furniture, (6) appliances, (7) clothing, and (8) medical services.

In the beauty parlor and dry cleaner categories, personal information was generally secured from representatives of local welcoming organizations. Co-workers, employers, and real estate representatives provided the majority of personal information on financial institutions. In the insurance area, company sales personnel typically provided the "personal" contact. Medical services were selected by sixty-eight families based on personal information from nonprofessional sources who were in the same age category, always married, generally of the same sex, and had similar incomes to families studied. Mobiles seeking medical information outside the immediate peer group tended to ask older women with larger families. Real estate personnel, new neighbors, and co-workers were all used to gain information about furniture and appliance outlets. While few mobiles bought new clothing in the first weeks of residence, when such decisions were made they rested upon the advice of co-workers and new friends. Typically, newly arrived mobiles did not regard neighbors as prime information sources.

Searching was instrumental in choosing supermarkets and played a secondary role in choices of dry cleaners, banks, furniture stores, appliance outlets, and clothing stores. However, as time in the community grew, searching declined in importance and mobiles relied increasingly upon personal conversations for the necessary answers.

Decision Responsibility

Findings revealed a clear division of decision responsibility among marriage partners. As expected, wives selected beauty parlors, and virtually all dress shops. In addition, wives made two-thirds of the supermarket and dry cleaning choices. Sole responsibility for selecting medical service suppliers rested with wives twice as often as husbands. Decisions by husbands were primarily confined to picking the family bank, insurance firms, and men's clothing stores. In mobile families, husbands, while being good providers, seemed to have delegated a majority of purchase decision responsibilities to wives. Joint decisions were the most common division of responsibility in only one purchase category —appliance stores. However, supermarket, medical service, furniture, and bank selections were also frequently made after mutual discussions.

Time Span to Selection and Suppliers Contacted

Mobiles tended to rebuild sources of supply rapidly. Overall, the mean time span varied from 1.0 weeks in selecting the first supermarket to 9.2 weeks in choosing a dentist. Mean values reveal that within six weeks, the majority of consumers making supplier choices in categories investigated had rebuilt a working shopping pattern. However, in the first six weeks following a change in residence few newcomers made purchases of clothing, automobiles, or life insurance. In most categories standard deviations from the means further pointed up the rapid pace at which new shopping patterns were established. As an identifiable market segment, mobiles disappeared within one month, and sooner in many purchase categories.

Number of Potential
Suppliers Visited

The findings on the average number of potential suppliers visited prior to the selection of a favorite supplier are shown in Table 4-1. In the case of supermarkets, beauty parlors, and dry cleaners the visits reflect actual transactions between the mobile families and various suppliers. In all other purchase categories

TABLE 4-1
Selection Pattern of Mobile Consumers

DECISION PATTERN

PURCHASE CATEGORY	Information Sources Used[1]	Main Family Decision Responsibility[2]	Weeks Between Arrival and Supplier Selection[3]	No. of Potential Suppliers Visited Prior to Choosing Favorites
Super-markets	30.0% Personal	66.0% Wife	1.0 weeks	
First	67.4% Searching	22.0% Joint		
	2.7% Im-personal	12.0% Husband		
	n = 147	n = 146	n = 147	
Favorite	38.6% Personal	66.0% Wife	3.4 weeks	3.4
	55.0% Searching	22.0% Joint		
	5.3% Im-personal	12.0% Husband	2.04*	
	n = 132	n = 139	n = 130	
Beauty parlors	72.7% Personal	100.0% Wife	5.0 Weeks	
First	17.3% Searching	Joint Husband	2.40*	
	10.0% Im-personal			
	n = 110	n = 128	n = 110	
Favorite	57.3% Personal	100.0% Wife	7.0 weeks	2.0
	37.5% Searching	Joint Husband	2.86*	
	5.2% Im-personal			
	n = 96	n = 106	n = 64	

[1]Percentages are based on the number of families making purchase in each category. All are based on the n shown.

[2]Percentages are based on the entire sample of 147. Families reported on how they had made decisions since moving and on how future purchase decisions would be made. n here refers to number of respondent answers.

[3]Reflects mean weeks taken to select suppliers.

*Reflects standard deviation from the mean.

n = number of frequencies used to calculate the mean and standard deviation.

DECISION PATTERN

Dry cleaners	76.3% Personal	62.2% Wife	3.7 weeks	
First	7.9% Searching	8.8% Joint		
	15.8% Impersonal	21.1% Husband	1.89*	
	n = 101	n = 137	n = 129	
Favorite	57.3% Personal	51.7% Wife	5.5 weeks	2.0
	37.5% Searching	9.5% Joint		
	5.2% Impersonal	16.3% Husband	1.75*	
	n = 96	n = 115	n = 97	
Financial institutions	51.0% Personal	4.8% Wife	1.7 weeks	1.0
Bank	43.0% Searching	25.0% Joint		
	6.0% Impersonal	65.0% Husband	1.68*	
	n = 127	n = 140	n = 134	
Savings and Loan	45.0% Personal	5.4% Wife	3.0 weeks	1.0
	20.0% Searching	7.5% Joint		
	35.0% Impersonal	33.4% Husband	2.26*	
	n = 20	n = 68	n = 22	
Credit union	100.0% Personal	3.4% Wife	4 weeks	2.0
	Searching Impersonal	7.5% Joint		
		35.0% Husband	3.45*	
	n = 25	n = 67	n = 23	
Insurance Auto-mobile	92.3% Personal	2.7% Wife	5.2 weeks	2.0
	0.0% Searching	10.0% Joint		
	7.7% Impersonal	53.0% Husband	4.18*	
	n = 121	n = 99	n = 29	

DECISION PATTERN

Insurance Property	95.5% Personal	2.7% Wife	2.7 weeks	1.0
	0.0% Searching	10.0% Joint		
	4.5% Im-personal	53.0% Husband	2.21*	
	n = 66	n = 107	n = 61	
Life	90.5% Personal	2.7% Wife	7.6 weeks	1.0
	0.0% Searching	11.6% Joint		
	9.5% Im-personal	41.5% Husband	4.46*	
	n = 21	n = 82	n = 22	
Furniture stores First	48.2% Personal	26.6% Wife	6.2 weeks	3.0
	21.7% Searching	21.8% Joint		
	30.1% Im-personal	8.0% Husband	2.94*	
	n = 83	n = 84	n = 81	
Second	47.1% Personal	15.6% Wife	6.4 weeks	3.6
	35.3% Searching	9.5% Joint		
	17.6% Im-personal	3.4% Husband	3.71*	
	n = 34	n = 42	n = 34	
Appliance stores First	62.0% Personal	11.6% Wife	5.3 weeks	2.0
	17.7% Searching	27.2% Joint		
	20.0% Im-personal	12.2% Husband	4.04*	
	n = 79	n = 75	n = 77	
Second	62.5% Personal	4.1% Wife	3.9 weeks	2.5
	25.0% Searching	6.8% Joint		
	12.5% Im-personal	5.4% Husband	2.35*	
	n = 16	n = 24	n = 15	

DECISION PATTERN

Clothing purchases	56.8% Personal	69.4% Wife	8.6 weeks	3.2
Women's better dresses	29.7% Searching	5.4% Joint		
	13.5% Im- personal	0.0% Husband	3.50*	
	n = 37	n = 111	n = 39	
Men's suits	65.0% Personal	4.8% Wife	8.3 weeks	2.2
	30.2% Searching	10.9% Joint		
	4.8% Im- personal	57.0% Husband	3.90*	
	n = 43	n = 108	n = 38	
Medical services	78.2% Personal	41.4% Wife	7.3 weeks	1.0
General practitioners	6.4% Searching	24.5% Joint		
	15.4% Im- personal	6.2% Husband	3.12*	
	n = 78	n = 107	n = 78	
Specialist	94.7% Personal	41.4% Wife	6.9 weeks	1.0
	0.0% Searching	24.5% Joint		
	5.3% Im- personal	6.2% Husband	2.86*	
	n = 75	n = 106	n = 68	
Dentist	86.5% Personal	42.2% Wife	9.2 weeks	1.0
	5.4% Searching	22.5% Joint		
	8.1% Im- personal	9.5% Husband	3.20*	
	n = 74	n = 109	n = 72	

the average number of potential suppliers visited reflects the number of suppliers contacted before the first purchase within a category was completed.

The research findings shown in Table A-1 reveal a variation in the number of contacts with potential suppliers from one in the medical service area to four in selecting a third furniture store. Supermarkets with 3.4 visits and women's clothing shops with 3.2 visits are other categories where over three potential suppliers were contacted. The table also reveals that mobiles tend to make few supplier selection decisions in the clothing area, choose few financial institutions other than banks, and purchase life and automobile insurance in less than 20 percent of the families.

Influence of Two Variables: Length of
Marriage and Age of Children upon
Decision Responsibility

Impact of Length of Marriage

A hypothesis was formulated stating that the length of time a couple had been married does not significantly influence the division of decision-making responsibility for choosing family suppliers.

The research findings reveal that families having joint decision responsibility for purchases typically have been married fewer years than families where the decision responsibility is assumed by either the husband or the wife. The above trend based upon a weighted average was found particularly in selecting supermarkets, financial institutions, medical services, and appliances. In none of the purchase categories investigated did the research findings statistically refute the hypothesis.

It was found that the length of time couples were married was not a significant factor in influencing the division of decision responsibility within the family. However, purchase decisions in which the husband and wife participated as equals were found most frequently in the couples that had been married less than ten years.

Impact of Children Five Years Old or Less

A hypothesis was developed relating to the influence children five years old or less have upon the decision responsibility of housewives in selection of family suppliers. The hypothesis stated that wives with one or more children five years old or less did not have significantly less responsibility in selecting suppliers than did wives in all other families.

The data reveal no overall differences in the decision-making roles of the wives in the two groups. However, in three purchase categories, supermarkets, automobile insurance, and the first men's suit supplier, wives with children five years old or less played a less important role than did other housewives.

Summary

Findings relating length of marriage to the assignment of decision responsibility revealed that in joint purchase decisions made by the husband and wife, the length of marriage was usually less than in families where purchase decisions were sole undertakings. In selecting financial institutions, the role of the husband appeared to increase as the years of marriage accumulated. In one area, furniture, where the wives play a major role, length of marriage tended to increase the role of the wife in decision making. The presence of children five years old or less did not appear to seriously diminish the role of housewives in decision making. In only three areas, the first supermarket, automobile insurance, and the first men's suit selection, did wives with children of five or less appear to play a smaller role in decision making than all other wives.

Impact of Income and Occupation

Income and Decision Responsibility

The hypothesis developed to test the relationship between income and decision responsibility stated that income is not a significant factor in the division of decision responsibility within a mobile family.

Families making joint purchases had the lowest incomes of all families in twelve of the twenty-one purchase categories investigated. In the same categories, when family purchase decisions were made by either the husband or wife, the family income was higher than that of families making joint decisions. Purchase categories exhibiting the pattern were: (1) first and (2) favorite supermarkets, (3) first and (4) favorite dry cleaners, (5) banks, (6) automobile insurance, (7) property insurance, (8) potential dress suppliers, (9) the first and (10) third furniture store, (11) the first and (12) second appliance store. Findings in the areas of general practitioners and men's suits deviated from the pattern. In these two categories the families using joint decisions had higher incomes than families where single decisions were made by either the husband or wife. In two purchase categories, the first and second furniture stores, the findings were found to be statistically significant. In these two areas wives typically made the supplier selection decisions in the higher income families.

Occupation and Decision
Responsibility

A hypothesis was formulated to study the relationship of occupation and decision responsibility. The hypothesis stated that the occupation of the head of a mobile family was not a significant factor in determining the division of decision-making responsibility within the family.

In three purchase categories: savings and loan firms, general practitioners, and furniture stores, findings statistically support the premise that the occupation of the household head affected the division of decision making within the mobile family. Husbands tended to have greater responsibility for selecting savings and loan firms in the higher occupational categories. On the other hand, they had less role in selecting general practitioners after reaching the more skillful occupations. In upper level occupations, husbands had little influence in selecting furniture stores. In other purchase categories investigated, study results exhibit a very similar division of decision responsibility among the various family members in all four occupational groups.

Summary

Research findings on the impact of income and occupation upon decision making supplement the data developed on life cycle variables. Findings relating income to the division of decision responsibility within families reveal that where husbands and wives made joint decisions incomes were typically less than that of families where decisions were made by one or the other mate. Research findings on the relationship of occupation to the division of decision responsibility reveal that in three purchase areas: savings and loan firms, general practitioners, and furniture stores, findings support the premise that the occupation of the household head affects the division of decision responsibility. In two purchase categories—general practitioners and furniture stores—wives gained responsibility as the occupational level of the household head declined. In savings and loan associations the reverse was found.

Selection of Information Sources

The study had two hypotheses to focus research on the relationship between educational level and information source. The first stated that there is not a significant relationship between the years of education of the head of a mobile family and the use of particular information sources in selecting family suppliers.

Findings indicate that each purchase category has a particular information source or sources which families prefer to use, regardless of educational level. The findings revealed a statistically significant relationship between the education of the husband and the use of particular information sources in selecting suppliers only in the selection of the family bank. In selecting banks, personal information sources tended to become of increasing importance as education increased. At the same time, searching declined as the educational level of the household increased.

The second hypothesis, dealing with education and source of information, stated no significant relationship existed between the education of the housewife in a mobile family and the use of particular information sources in selecting family suppliers. As was established in the previous hypothesis, the findings suggest that each purchase category has a favorite information source or sources which families use regardless of educational level in selecting suppliers. In the selection of banks, savings and loan firms, automobile insurance, women's dress suppliers, men's suit stores, and general practitioners, research findings tend to indicate a relationship exists between the use of particular information sources and the housewives educational level. Personal information was relatively more important to the wives on the lower educational levels. In other purchase categories the research did not reveal a significant relationship between the selection of particular information sources used in choosing suppliers and the educational level of the housewife.

Occupation and Source of Information

The third hypothesis developed to focus the research study on factors affecting the selection of information sources stated that the occupation of the head of a mobile family was not a significant factor in determining the information sources used in selecting suppliers for family needs.

Overall, the research findings failed to support the premise that a relationship exists between occupation and the selection of information sources in the areas investigated. In the selection of a potential beauty parlor, however, the results proved to be statistically significant. Use of information sources appeared to be similar in each of the occupational categories. The research did not verify a relationship between occupation and the use of particular information sources in selecting suppliers.

Income and Information Source Usage

Formulation of the fourth hypothesis was based upon the premise that the income of a mobile family was not a significant factor in determining the information sources used in selecting suppliers. In the selection of a dentist, the findings support the premise that a significant relationship exists between average family income and type of information used in selecting suppliers.

The relationship was not found to be significant in any other purchase category.

Families per Dwelling and Information Source Usage

The fifth hypothesis stated that whether a family resided in a one family or a multi-family dwelling was not a significant factor in determining the information sources used in selecting suppliers. The findings failed to establish an overall relationship between the use of particular information sources and whether a family resided in a one family or a multi-family dwelling. Only in the purchase of property insurance did the findings reveal a statistically significant difference between the information sources used and whether a family resided in a one family or a multi-family dwelling. Here the findings need to be evaluated in light of the small number (nine) of families residing in multi-family dwellings purchasing property insurance.

Summary

Findings on the relationship between education and information source usage revealed that each purchase category has a particular information source or sources which mobile families prefer to use regardless of education. Only in the selection of a bank was a relationship found between the educational level of the household head and the use of particular information sources in selecting a supplier. Personal information was used more often as the educational level increased.

Findings on the relationship of the educational level of the housewife and the selection of suppliers showed a relationship in the following areas: banks, savings and loans, automobile insurance, women's dress suppliers, men's suit stores, and general practitioners. Personal information was found to be relatively more important to wives on lower educational levels.

Research findings on the relationship of occupation to the use of information sources in selecting suppliers failed to reveal an overall relationship between the two factors. Information sources used to select suppliers tended to be the same in each of the occupational categories. Income was found to be a determining factor in the use of information in only one purchase category: the selection of a dentist.

Research findings on whether the number of families per dwelling had an effect upon the type of information used in selecting suppliers showed a significant relationship in only one area: property insurance. Personal information was used by virtually all the one family dwelling residents in buying property insurance.

Impact of Education Level and Past Moves upon the Time Taken to Select Suppliers

Educational Level and Time Taken to Select Suppliers

Two hypotheses were formulated to study the relationship between educational level and the time taken to select new suppliers.

The first hypothesis stated that a significant relationship did not exist between the educational level of the household head and the weeks taken to select favorite suppliers after completing a long distance move. Only in the average number of weeks taken to select a bank did the study results show a statistically significant relationship between the level of education attained by a household head and the time taken to select a supplier. In the selection of a bank the process was more rapid as the average level of education increased.

The second hypothesis stated that a significant relationship existed between the educational level of the mobile housewife and the weeks taken to select her favorite suppliers. As in the previous hypothesis, the overall findings did not show a significant relationship. Only in the purchase category of life insurance did the findings reveal a statistically significant relationship between education of housewives and the time taken to select new suppliers.

In families where housewives had at least some college education, less time was taken in selecting life insurance suppliers than in families where the wife had less education.

The final hypothesis was formulated to study the impact of the number of long distance moves a family had made in the past decade upon the time taken to select suppliers upon completion of a long distance move. Specifically, the hypothesis stated that a significant relationship did not exist between the number of long distance moves a family had made in the past decade and the weeks taken to select favorite suppliers after completing a long distance move. In the selection of the first furniture store used by a family upon arrival in a community, findings revealed a statistically significant relationship between the number of moves a family had made in the past decade and the time taken to select the store. Families making the first long distance move typically did less shopping around and made their initial purchases soon after arrival.

In all of the other purchase categories investigated the research findings fail to substantiate the premise that the number of moves a family had made in the past played a role in the time it took a family to select suppliers after completion of a move. Experienced movers took as long to select new suppliers as families making their first long distance move.

Summary

Research on the possible relationship between education and the time taken to select new suppliers dealt with the education of both the husband and wife. Findings relating the educational level of the husband and the time taken to select suppliers revealed that in selecting banks the process was more rapid as the average level of education increased. Findings relating the educational level of the housewife and the time taken to select new suppliers revealed a relationship in the selection of life insurance suppliers.

The research findings, pertaining to the relationship of the time taken to select new suppliers and the number of long distance moves completed by a family during the past decade, reveal that in selecting the first furniture store the process was more rapid in families experiencing fewer moves. In the other purchase categories the research results did not show a statistically significant relationship.

This study developed a body of knowledge tangential to the prime research thrust in addition to data specifically pertaining to the research hypotheses.

Selection of Suppliers

Table 4-2 contains a summary of the reasons given by mobiles for selecting suppliers. Mobiles indicated convenience was the most important factor in selecting suppliers. Specific reasons for their selections in each category provide clues to the selection process. Seventy and seven-tenths of the selection reasons were centered in these six categories: (1) convenience, 19.6 percent; (2) familiarity, 12.4 percent; (3) recommendations, 10.3 percent; (4) quality of work or merchandise, 9.8 percent; (5) low prices, 9.7 percent; and (6) service, 8.9 percent.

Within each purchase category a particular reason was found to be of prime importance. Convenience was the most important factor in selecting supermarkets, dry cleaners, and financial institutions. Variety was the major reason given for selecting furniture and appliance stores and suppliers of men's suits and women's better dresses and suits. In selecting insurance, familiarity of the firm or the fact that families had done business before with the firm were the prime reasons given. In choosing suppliers of medical services the findings indicate that personal sources of information were of prime importance, and were used in over 50 percent of the selection decisions. Beauty parlors were the only supply category where promotion played the

TABLE 4-2

Reasons Given by Mobile Families for Selecting Initial and Favorite Suppliers in Each Purchase Category

PURCHASE CATEGORIES

Reasons Given for Selection		Supermarkets	Beauty Parlors	Dry Cleaners	Financial Institutions	Insurance	Furniture and Appliances	Men's Suits and Women's Better Dresses	Medical Services	Total All Categories
Convenient location	n	147	31	97	102	0	8	0	31	416
	%	25.7*	18.2	33.1*	43.7*	0.0	3.1	0.0	17.3	19.6
Familiar firm or family did business with this firm in prior community	n	36	4	0	35	142	30	5	10	262
	%	6.3	2.3	0.0	15.1	41.9*	11.6	7.4	5.6	12.4
Recommendation of friends, neighbors, relatives or professional sources	n	0	19	12	25	54	12	2	94	218
	%	0.0	11.1	4.1	10.8	15.9	4.6	2.9	52.5*	10.3
Low prices	n	96	4	0	10	50	36	9	0	205
	%	16.8	2.3	0.0	4.3	14.7	13.9	13.2	0.0	9.7
Service	n	40	6	60	6	29	18	0	29	188
	%	7.0	3.5	20.5	2.6	8.6	7.0	0.0	16.2	8.9
Variety	n	42	0	0	0	0	61	39	0	142
	%	7.3	0.0	0.0	0.0	0.0	23.6*	57.3*	0.0	6.7
Promotion	n	12	47	59	0	0	11	0	0	129
	%	2.1	27.5*	20.1	0.0	0.0	4.2	0.0	0.0	6.1
Quality of merchandise sold or work performed	n	93	45	43	0	0	20	5	0	206
	%	16.3	26.3	14.7	0.0	0.0	7.7	7.4	0.0	9.8
Familiar brands available	n	34	0	0	0	0	27	0	0	61
	%	5.9	0.0	0.0	0.0	0.0	10.4	0.0	0.0	2.9
Relative or friend works at firm	n	0	0	0	4	28	4	0	0	36
	%	0.0	0.0	0.0	1.7	8.3	1.5	0.0	0.0	1.7
Physical facility	n	28	0	0	3	0	0	0	0	31
	%	4.9	0.0	0.0	1.3	0.0	0.0	0.0	0.0	1.5
Credit established	n	0	0	0	20	0	9	0	0	29
	%	0.0	0.0	0.0	8.9	0.0	3.5	0.0	0.0	1.4
Other	n	44	15	22	27	36	23	8	15	190
	%	7.7	8.8	7.5	11.6	7.0	8.9	11.8	8.4	9.0
Total all categories	n	572	171	293	232	339	259	68	179	2113
	%	100.0	100.0	100.0	100.0	100.0	100.0	100.0	100.0	100.0

*Indicates reason given most frequently for a purchase category.

major role in the selection process; the quality of work performed was a close second.

Reasons for Not Selecting
Initial Suppliers as
Favorite Suppliers

Table 4-3 presents the findings on three purchase categories in which the mobile families interviewed had made a number of purchases in supermarkets, beauty shops, and dry cleaners. The Table reveals the reasons given for not selecting initial suppliers as favorite family suppliers. Poor quality of merchandise or service accounted for 32.7 percent of the reasons. High prices accounted for 27.1 percent, and poor appearance of personnel or store, 11.1 percent. Inconvenience was found to be the major factor in 9.3 percent of the non-selection instances.

TABLE 4-3

Reasons Given by Mobile Families for Not Selecting the First
Supplier as the Favorite Supplier in Three Purchases

Reasons For Not Selecting	Super-markets		Beauty Parlors		Dry Cleaners		Totals	
	number	percent	number	percent	number	percent	number	percent
Poor quality of merchandise or service	11	22.9	29	45.4	13	26.0	53	32.7
High prices	19	39.5	7	10.9	18	36.0	44	27.1
Poor appearance of personnel or store	3	6.3	15	23.4	0	0.0	18	11.1
Inconvenient	7	14.6	0	0.0	8	16.0	15	9.3
Other	8	16.7	13	20.3	11	22.0	32	19.8
TOTAL	48	100.0	64	100.0	50	100.0	162	100.0

Influence of Trading Stamps on
the Selection of Supermarkets

Tables 4-4 and 4-5 present the research findings pertaining to the importance of trading stamps in the selection of food suppliers for mobile families. The results show that 81 percent of the mobile families saved trading stamps. Results also reveal that 64.6 percent of the families did the first major food shopping, after moving, in stores giving stamps. Twenty-five families indicated that trading stamps influenced the selection of a first

TABLE 4-4

Influence of Trading Stamps on the Selection of Food Stores by Mobile Families

Category of Stamp Usage	Number	Extent of Trading Stamp Usage by Mobile Families			
		Yes		No	
		Percent	Number	Percent	
Do mobile families save trading stamps? 119		81.0	28	19.0	
Did the first major local food shopping of mobile families take place in a food store giving stamps? 95		64.6	52	35.4	
Did trading stamps influence the selection of a first or favorite food store? 25		17.0	122	83.0	

TABLE 4-5

How Trading Stamps Influenced Twenty-Five Families

Reasons for Influencing	Number	Percentage
Like to save stamps 13		52.0
Save them if given—no influence................ 5		20.0
Don't like stamps 4		16.0
Shop where there are low prices no stamps given 3		12.0
TOTALS 25		100.0

or favorite supermarket. Of the twenty-five families, thirteen felt stamps were a positive influence in the selection of a food store.

Influence of Credit upon
the Purchase Decisions
of Mobile Families

Each housewife interviewed was asked to identify three charge accounts the family had been able to transfer to stores in the new community. Housewives reported, on an average, less than one transferred charge account per family. The accounts transferred were with two retailers in 78.1 percent of the transfers. A complete breakdown of transferred charge accounts is presented in Table 4-6.

TABLE 4-6

Influence of Credit upon Purchase
Decisions of Mobile Families

Firm	Transferred Charge Accounts	
	Number	Percentage
Sears, Roebuck	69	53.9
J. C. Penney	31	24.2
Montgomery Ward	4	3.1
W. T. Grant	2	1.6
S. S. Kresge	2	1.6
Others	20	15.6
TOTAL	128	100.0

Table 4-7 presents the research findings on the use of the transferred charge accounts. It reveals that of the 128 reported as transferred, nearly 80.0 percent were used in the new community.

TABLE 4-7

Use of Transferred Charge Accounts

	Number	Percentage
Families using transferred charge accounts......	102	79.7
Families not using transferred charge accounts...	26	20.3
TOTAL	128	100.0

Table 4-8 presents the findings on use of credit by mobile families in making 244 furniture and appliance purchases; 48.0 percent of the purchases were made on credit. The Table also reveals that the use of credit of the families studied declined as the purchase frequency increased.

Research findings on the types of suppliers at which families opened charge accounts are in Table 4-9. Of the new accounts, 55.3 percent were opened at department stores. Of all the accounts opened, 31.8 percent were initiated at two local department stores, while 14 percent of the new accounts were with the local outlet of one national department store organization. Ap-

TABLE 4-8

Use of Credit by Mobile Families Making 244 Furniture and Appliance Purchases[a]

Nature of Purchase	Cash		Method of Payment Charge		Total	
	number	percent	number	percent	number	percent
APPLIANCES						
First appliance store	41	51.2	39	48.8	80	85.0
Second appliance store	14	54.0	12	46.0	26	15.0
Sub Total	55	58.4	51	41.6	106	100.0
FURNITURE						
First furniture store	44	52.4	40	47.6	84	60.8
Second furniture store	20	45.5	22	54.5	44	31.9
Third furniture store	8	80.0	2	20.0	10	7.3
Sub Total	72	52.2	64	47.8	138	100.0
TOTAL 127		52.0	115	48.0	244	100.0

a. 111 of the 147 families purchases at least one appliance or one piece of furniture. The total expenditure for all families was $91,615.00. The average for all 147 families was $623.33 per family.

TABLE 4-9

Types of Suppliers at Which Mobile Families Opened New Charge Accounts After Moving

Type of Store	Accounts Opened Number	Percentage
DEPARTMENT STORES		
Local organizations (2)	57	38.1
National organizations (1)	21	14.0
Regional organizations (1)	5	3.3
	(83)	(55.4)
Men's apparel stores (3)	20	13.3
Women's apparel stores (5)	15	10.0
Furniture stores (2)	6	4.0
Gasoline companies (1)	5	3.3
Others	21	14.0
TOTAL 150		100.0

parel stores were second in importance to the department stores in terms of the number of new accounts opened. Men's and women's apparel stores accounted for 23.3 percent of the total account openings.

Impact of Carry Over on
Supplier Selections

Table 4-10 presents the research findings on the impact of past experience upon the selection of suppliers by mobile families. Previous experience was listed as most important in the selection of insurance suppliers, with 41.9 percent of all insurance purchases selected based upon previous experience. In the selection of furniture and appliance suppliers, previous experience was the major factor in 25.5 percent of the purchases. In

TABLE 4-10

Impact of Previous Experience or Carry Over upon the
Selection of Suppliers by Mobile Families

Type of Previous Experience	Food[a]		Number and Percent of Carry Over Reasons or Total Reasons Given for Selection Purchase Areas Furniture & Appliances		Insurance		Financial Institutions	
	n	%	n	%	n	%	n	%
Previous experience with firm	11	1.9	30	11.6	115	32.4	35	14.9
Familiar name	25	4.4	0	0.0	27	9.5	0	0.0
Credit established	0	0.0	9	3.5	0	0.0	0	0.0
Familiar brands	34	5.6	27	10.4	0	0.0	0	0.0
Total	70	11.9	66	25.5	142	41.9	35	14.9

[a]Sixty-six of the 147 families or 45.0 percent did the first major food shopping at a store having the same name as one patronized or recognized from a prior community. Only fifty-two families or 36.7 percent selected favorite supermarkets having the same names as one doing business in their prior communities.

the selection of financial institutions, experience was the major factor in thirty-five or 14.9 percent of all reasons given. Mobile families indicated previous experience was a prime reason for selecting a food store in only 11.9 percent of the total reasons given. However, 45.0 percent of the families did the first major local food shopping at the store recognized from previous experience. In the selection of men's suits and women's better dresses and suits, prior experience was given as a reason 6.9 percent of the time. The transfer of 128 charge accounts in Table 4-6 shows another role of previous experience in family purchase decisions.

Summary of Other Findings

The major importance of convenience in the selection process by which mobile families choose new suppliers was indicated in this study. Convenience was followed in importance by the value mobile families attached to familiarity with firms, and also by the use made of personal recommendations. Following these prime factors, the reasons for selection were found to be familiarity, recommendations, quality, low prices, and service.

Variety, promotion, familiarity of brands, and other factors were also indicated as reasons.

Research findings on the reasons for not selecting initial suppliers as favorite suppliers revealed that poor quality of merchandise or service were the major factors. High prices were the second most frequently listed reason. Poor appearance of personnel or store, and inconvenience, were two other less frequently listed reasons for not selecting the first supplier as the favorite.

Trading stamps were saved by 81 percent of the mobile families. Stamps played a role in the selection of food suppliers in twenty-five families or 17 percent of the families studied. Stamps were a positive influence in slightly over one-half of the twenty-five families.

Housewives interviewed on the use of credit by mobile families reported that 128 accounts had been transferred into the new community. Nearly 80 percent of the accounts transferred were used. Of the 128 accounts transferred, 78.1 percent were with two national general merchandise organizations. The mobile families used credit in 48.0 percent of the reported furniture and and appliance purchases.

Previous experience with a firm was also a factor to evaluate. In the insurance category, past experience was given as a reason for selection in 41.9 percent of all purchases. Experience was also given as a major reason in the selection of furniture and appliance suppliers. In the selection of financial institutions and food stores, experience was also an important factor. Sixty-six families, or 45 percent of the families studied, made the initial local food purchases in stores recognizable from experience gained in prior localities.

V

Summary and Conclusions

Identification of the Long Distance Mobile Market

The long distance mobile market was found to be composed of well educated, white collar professional or managerial families, earning above average incomes and having children at home. The income and occupation of the household heads in these families reflected levels which were commensurate with education well over the national average. More than 66 percent of the household heads and more than 40 percent of the housewives had completed college. An indication of the high educational level of mobile families was the fact that 40.2 percent of the household heads had completed some postgraduate work. In contrast to the sample, only 18 percent of the nation's population over twenty-five years of age had attained an educational level equivalent to some college work in 1965.[1]

Long distance mobiles expected to receive incomes substantially higher than average for 1966. Families interviewed expected a median income of $10,000 to $14,999. The figure was appreciably higher than the national median income of $6,566 reported for all households in 1964.[2] It also was above the approximated $9,600 effective buying income reported for the metropolitan area under study for 1965.[3]

58

Eighty percent of the mobile household heads had occupations in professional and managerial categories. Only 25.6 percent of all the males in the nation held occupations in these two categories at the time of the 1960 census.[4] Slightly over 10 percent of the sample household heads held blue collar jobs.

Mobile families had, on the average, been married eleven years when the survey was conducted. The presence of one or more children under five years in two-thirds of the families reflected the relative youth of the family units.

Housewives drove an automobile in over 95 percent of the families, and families had an average of 1.7 automobiles available. In nearly 75 percent of the families, wives had an automobile available for use when the husband was absent from home.

Based on the research, mobile housewives worked outside the home for pay in slightly more than 10 percent of the families; those working outside the home were primarily part-time workers.

Mobile families have a high tendency to make additional long distance moves. On the average, each family in the nation makes one long distance move every sixteen years. The mobile families interviewed had experienced one long distance move every three years. With a rate of mobility of one move every three years, they had a long distance mobility rate nearly five times the national average. Not all of the mobiles had made a long distance move prior to the one bringing the family into the study area; one-third of the families had not made a previous long distance move.

Based on prior residence, two-thirds of the mobile families had come from out of state or from overseas. The remaining one-third had moved within the study state. When moving into the study community over 80 percent of the mobiles moved into one family dwellings. Ownership of the place of residence was assumed by 55 percent of the families.

Impact of Sample Homogeneity
upon Research Findings

The sample upon which the study was based was concentrated in relatively narrow categories of income, occupation, and education. In addition, the families interviewed tended to reside in similar types of dwellings. Because of the relatively homogeneous nature of the sample, it was difficult to determine the impact of varying socio-economic characteristics upon family decision making. The homogeneity was most apparent in the cluster of incomes expected for 1966. The mean, median, and mode income were all in the same category: $10,000 to $14,999.

Similarity of the mobile market contributed to the general support given the null hypotheses. If the families had been a more heterogeneous group, a greater number of the null hypotheses might have been rejected. The research findings offer support to the premise that a relatively homogeneous sample of families could be expected to exhibit similar patterns of conduct. In establishing the homogeneity of the market segment the research did verify the uniqueness of the market. While the similarity of long distance mobiles may have nullified the opportunity to disprove the research hypotheses, it clearly established the homogeneous nature of the long distance mobile market. The prime research objective, to test the established hypotheses, was carried out successfully.

Positive Aspects of Homogeneity

The purpose of the concept of market segmentation, to determine differences among buyers which may be consequential in marketing, played a key role in this research. In establishing the homogeneous nature of a large, identifiable, and affluent mobile market segment the research provided valuable data for marketers. The ultimate benefit of segmentation based upon mobility is tied to the degree to which mobiles moving into various markets are similar. Verification of similar socio-economic characteristics in independent samples will provide a basis for predicting buyer behavior.

In the research conducted by Andreasen the long distance mobile group was found to be superior to the rest of the population according to four criteria: present spending power, potential for future increased spending power, present purchase behavior, and potential for change in future purchase behavior.[5] The study by Andreasen was made with 148 geographic mobiles. An analysis of the socio-economic characteristics of his sample revealed a marked similarity with the profile of families in this research study. In the work by Andreasen, mobiles were also found to be concentrated in the managerial or professional occupations, to have above average educations, and to be earning higher than average incomes.

The similar median incomes of $10,000 to $15,000 for both samples indicated the homogeneous nature of the long distance-mobile market.[6] In addition, both studies found that long distance mobiles had typically made a number of long distance moves.[7]

In Andreasen's study 70 percent of the household heads had attended college. Mobile household heads in 80 percent of the families interviewed in this research had attended college. The difference can be partially explained by the presence of a major university in the study research area. A number of mobile household heads had moved to the community to join the university's faculty.

Both this study and Andreasen's have identified the similar nature of the long distance mobile market. Mobiles would appear to exhibit similar socio-economic patterns independent of the destination of the move. The market identified for suppliers and manufacturers has been described in such detail that marketing efforts may be more precisely directed toward the area of opportunity.

The benefits of segmenting the market are that promotions may be directed at specific individuals, timed for maximum efficiency, and adjusted to meet distinguishable changes in the market. In the search for broad classes of buyers distinguishable from the mass market, this research has made a positive contribution to marketing by further segmenting the mass market. The usefulness of identifying the mobile market for specific programs is enhanced by the relative ease by which the location, size, and affluence of the market can be measured. Because of the unique character of mobility, the market is accessible for focusing marketing efforts. The homogeneity of the market is a key dimension in the process. The size and affluence of the market further substantiate the benefits of the research which has provided additional information on the unique nature of a segment of the consumer market.

A Managerial Strategy for Marketing to Mobile Families

Changes in residence by nearly 20 percent of the nation's population each year makes possible the segmentation of over 36 million individuals based upon geographic mobility. Identification of the mobile segment is of particular value in marketing to the over 13 million individuals making long distance moves annually. The long distance mobiles comprise a market larger in size than the state of Pennsylvania.

Long distance mobiles comprise an important market segment not only because of size, but also due to the economic power of the market segment. The power may be traced to high levels of education attained by mobiles and the nature of their occupations. The cluster of their incomes in the $10,000 to $15,000 category identifies the market as having above average potential for marketers. Because of the high repetitive mobility rate of long distance mobiles, identification of the market segment has additional value beyond the geographic confines of a single trading area. People moving into one area and losing their identification as mobiles after a number of weeks in a community can be expected to rejoin the mobile segment in another community within three or four years.

The Steps in Segmentation

The process of showing that mobiles are a distinct market segment involved four distinct steps: identification of the market, a study of market homogeneity, investigation of the accessibility of the market, and an estimate of market potential.[8]

The first step, the identification of the overall market segment based upon geographic mobility, has been done for several years by the U.S. Bureau of Census and indicates the mobility of nearly 20 percent of the nation's population. In addition, the reports made by the bureau for a decade showed that each year the breakdown of mobiles by-distance-moved remained relatively constant.

The second step, involving studies on the degree of homogeneity among the mobiles, was accomplished in part by the research study and by Andreasen's work. Both studies found that long distance movers are very similar in terms of socio-economic and life cycle characteristics.

The third step in segmentation investigated the accessibility of the mobile market for promotional efforts. Based on the research, the long distance mobile market would appear to be accessible for some time after the completion of a long distance move. The nature of a move and the associated disruptions of family life tended to make mobiles relatively accessible and receptive to promotional efforts aimed at helping families in rebuilding shopping patterns.

As the final step toward segmentation, the mobile market potential for specific firms should be determined. Estimation of the potential market should include an evaluation of the benefits to a firm of allocating resources to the mobile market and a comparison of the expected revenues to other alternative uses of promotional dollars. In the process, each firm ought to evaluate the relative potential of the mobile market in the trading area served and compare the possible returns to alternative marketing programs.

Strategies for Suppliers

Firms have three broad strategy alternatives in terms of the mobile market. They can make no attempt at developing a different program for the market, develop special programs aimed at the mobile market segment (while maintaining regular programs for the core market customers), or concentrate entirely upon the mobile market segment.

Firms operating on the premise that no attempt will be made at developing programs specifically for the mobile segment may assume that regular programs will reach mobiles. For example, a department store may decide not to advertise directly to mobiles or to encourage mobiles to open charge accounts. Such a firm might assume that regular advertising and a large clientele will draw mobiles to the store.

Other firms may decide to structure the total marketing program to include a separate plan for marketing to mobiles while retaining programs aimed at core market customers. A third alternative, that of marketing entirely to mobiles, would be a strategy likely to be adopted by firms associated with uprooting, moving, and settling mobile families into new residences.

Supermarkets

Mobiles interviewed in this study usually did their first major local food shopping at the most convenient supermarket. Forty-five percent of this shopping was done in stores having the same name as stores patronized prior to moving into the study area. Wives alone made the initial food store selection in nearly 70 percent of the families. Husbands alone made about 10 percent of the decisions and participated in joint decision with their wives in over 20 percent of the families. Families learned about the first food store used primarily through making a search of the area near home.

After mobiles had been in the community for three or four weeks, visits had usually been made to three or four competing outlets. Following the visits, 90 percent of the families identified one or more food stores as a favorite family supplier. The selection of favorite food suppliers was usually done by the wife alone or by the wife with some help from her husband. While the initial supermarkets were selected primarily because of convenience, favorite stores were identified primarily because of merchandising policies. Such factors as price, variety, familiarity of brands, and particularly the quality of produce and meat accounted for nearly 60 percent of all selection reasons. Quality of meat and produce alone accounted for 20 percent of the reasons given for identifying particular outlets as preferred suppliers. In the study area, the favorite food store selected was more likely to be a national chain (38.8 percent), or a regional chain (27.9 percent), than a locally owned outlet (23.1 percent). Families moving into the study area tended to increase patronage in regional chains at the expense of national chains after getting adjusted to the community. When families selected stores other than the ones initially visited as favorite suppliers the chief causes of dissatisfaction were high prices, poor service, and inconvenience.

More than 80 percent of the mobile families saved trading stamps. Sixty-five percent indicated that the first local food store shopping was done in stores giving stamps. Twenty-five of the families studied stated trading stamps had influenced their selection of a food store. Slightly more than half of the twenty-five families indicated that stamps were a positive factor in the selection of food suppliers.

When families selected more than one favorite food store the distribution of purchases was typically to spend from 70 to 80 percent of the food budget with the favorite supplier, about 15 percent with the second favorite supplier, and the remainder with the third supplier. Few interviewed could recall an attempt by a food retailer doing business in the study area to ask for their patronage.

In developing marketing programs for mobile consumers food retailers should gear their efforts to the first three weeks a new family lives in the community. After a three week period the selection process is usually completed and the mobile market segment has been assimilated into the total market. Particular attention should be devoted to adjusting the mobile food marketing programs to the housewife because decisions on the selection of stores are usually made by the housewife. Direct mail and personal contacts might profitably be used in contacting newcomers.

Reasons given by mobiles for dissatisfaction with food retailers, primarily poor quality of meat and produce, offer logical clues for development of a marketing strategy. Evidence in the trading area studied pointed to a particular need for newcomer promotion programs for locally-owned and operated firms. Mobiles had a marked tendency to use a familiar outlet when doing their first local food shopping. While the strong market position of national and regional chain firms in the area studied could account for the concentration of mobile food purchases, it also shows the need for firms having a relatively small marketing area to promote in the mobile market segment.

Efforts to tie mobiles to a particular food retailer could profitably include check cashing services for the newcomers. Such a program might also include a special introductory gift package of private label items which could be picked up at the market over a two or three week period. Having the store manager personally authorize the check cashing or distribution of the gift items would appear to be additional ways to personalize the store to newcomers.

Dry Cleaners

Dry cleaners were used by 89.1 percent of the mobile families interviewed. The initial dry cleaning was typically done during their third week of residence in the community and generally was done in a conventional operation. The cleaning was taken to the firm performing the work by two-thirds of the families; pick up and delivery services were used by the remaining one-third of the families.

Mobile families relied primarily upon personal information sources and searching in gathering information about potential cleaners. Specifically, the personal information sources used were recommendations from various welcoming services and suggestions from other individuals. In the searching process newcomers typically selected the cleaners most convenient to home or work. The responsibility for selecting the initial cleaner was found to be that of the housewife in over 60 percent of the families; the husband alone assumed the responsibility in 21.1 percent of the families. The primary reasons given for selecting initial dry cleaners were: convenience to home (28.8 percent), convenience to work (7.1 percent), and receipt of coupons given by a welcoming organization (27.6 percent).

Favorite dry cleaners were selected by nearly two-thirds of the mobile families. Cleaners designated as family favorites were typically chosen during the fifth week of residence in the community and after each family had used the dry cleaning service of two competing firms. Assignment of the responsibility for selecting favorite dry cleaners was found to be very similar to the pattern developed in selecting initial cleaners. Personal sources of information were used in selecting over one-half of the favorite dry cleaners. Searching for the most convenient location was used in about one-third of the selection processes.

Prime reasons given by mobiles for selecting specific dry cleaners as their favorites were: good work, good service, and convenience of location. Fifty, or nearly 40 percent of the families interviewed did not select the first dry cleaner used as the family favorite. Reasons for this, in order of importance, were: too expensive, poor work, and too far away. Close to 90 percent of the newcomers selecting favorite dry cleaners had the work done by conventional dry cleaning methods. Slightly over one-third of the mobiles had the favorite cleaner pick up and deliver the cleaning.

The marketing program of a dry cleaning establishment aimed specifically at mobile families might start with personal calls upon the housewife. During the call, whether by a welcoming organization or by a routeman, the housewife could be given a coupon for dry cleaning a garment. In particular, the initial coupon should be a vehicle for demonstrating the quality of workmanship and service available from the cleaner and probably not tied to a price reduction on the cleaning of one garment.

The use of personal contacts at home is one way for a dry cleaning firm with a limited number of outlets to extend its trading area. However, firms with numerous locations would also benefit by personally contacting newcomers. Since only one-third of the mobiles made use of a pick up and delivery service, the ability of a firm to extend the trading area served through using pick up and delivery services would be somewhat dependent upon changing customer habits. Routemen should be trained to search for and contact all new families.

While wives play the major role in selecting dry cleaners, promotion to the head of the mobile household should not be neglected. Husbands in mobile families typically wear clothing needing dry cleaning to work and frequently select cleaners close to their place of employment. Identification of household heads would be an important part of an overall program aimed at mobiles.

Promotions aimed at winning the dry cleaning business of newcomers should be made as soon as the families are identifiable and promotional efforts concentrated during their first five weeks in the community. The prime complaints of newcomers on the first cleaner used would appear to offer a basis for preparing an overall strategy for the mobile market. Initial contacts should provide the mobile family with an opportunity to test a firm's work, judge the service offered, and possibly determine the price levels. Being frequent users of dry cleaning services, mobiles tend to be very aware of price levels. A plan cleaners might use in winning the patronage of mobile families might be a promotion program geared to discounts on volume purchases and tied to opening a charge account.

Beauty Parlors

Beauty parlors were used by three-quarters of the mobile

housewives interviewed within twenty weeks of their arrival. Selection of beauty parlors was almost the exclusive responsibility of the housewife, who generally learned about the first local beauty parlor she used through a visit by a local welcoming organization or through the personal recommendation of another housewife. The two information sources accounted for nearly 75 percent of the initial consumer intelligence on beauty parlors. On the average, housewives had been in the commnuity nearly a month before making their first visit to a beauty parlor.

While the first beauty parlors used were usually selected because free coupons had been given to the newcomer by a welcoming organization, or because a friend recommended the shop, the reasons for selection of favorites were quite different. Good work and good service were the reasons given (by 70 percent) for selecting favorite beauty parlors; sixty-four of the housewives interviewed did not select the first beauty shop used as the favorite. This means that nearly 60 percent of the initial hair care received by mobile families was not considered adequate. The dissatisfaction was primarily attributed to the following: poor appearance of shops and operators (23.5 percent), poor styling (20.3 percent), poor service (15.6 percent), and high prices (10.9 percent).

The selection of a favorite beauty parlor had been made by sixty-four families or nearly 45 percent of the sample. The selection was made on an average 5.5 weeks after arrival and after visits had been made to two local beauty parlors.

In developing a marketing program for beauty parlors oriented to the mobile housewife, two factors are of prime concern. The first deals with informing newcomers of the availability of the service; the second with providing a satisfactory service so the customer will return. The information process should include personal contacts with the housewife. An important part of such a program might be providing the newcomer with some inducement, such as a price reduction, to try the service.

Promotions for hair care directed at mobile housewives should be initiated shortly after a family has moved into a community.

The second week of residence would appear to be an ideal contact time. Use of the mass media does not appear to be a logical way to reach the market. Personal contact, followed by good service in a clean establishment, would appear to be the best means to attract the mobile housewife.

Financial Institutions

One or more new bank accounts were opened by 134 (or 90 percent) of the 147 mobile families studied. The first account opened at a local bank was typically initiated during the first ten days of a family's residence in the community. The account was a checking account in over 90 percent of the new account openings. After mobile families had been in the community a number of weeks a second bank account was opened by slightly over 40 percent of the families. The second account was typically a savings account.

Mobile families gave 183 reasons for their selection of various banks. Forty-one percent listed convenience to home as the chief reason; 18 percent gave previous experience with the firm as the more important factor, and 10 percent listed "convenient to place of employment" as their prime reason.

Husbands made bank selections alone in nearly two-thirds of the families and were helped by wives in another third of the selection decisions. Mobile families relied heavily upon personal sources of information (51 percent), and upon searching (42 percent), in selecting banks.

Savings and loan accounts were opened by twenty-two of the mobile families after moving to the study area. Information on firms selected was acquired primarily from personal sources and, to a lesser extent, from the mass media. Savings and loan firms were selected on an average between the second and fourth week of residence in the community. Only one firm was usually visited in the selection process. Savings and loan firms were selected primarily because a home was financed through the firm or the firm was convenient to the home of the mobile family.

Accounts at local credit unions were opened by twenty-three mobile families. The accounts were generally opened four weeks after families arrived in the community. Decisions on the selection of credit unions were primarily the responsibility of the husbands. Families learned about all the credit unions selected through the contact with employers. Accounts were opened at credit unions primarily to secure loans.

Slightly over 40 percent of the mobile families received a loan of one type or another since moving to the community. Banks were identified as the loan source by 38.5 percent of the families, while credit unions were identified as a loan source by 27 percent of the group. Savings and loan firms were used by 13 percent of the families. In response to questions asking what sources would be used for automobile loans, $500.00 cash loans, and home loans, mobile families generally identified banks and credit unions. The two sources accounted for nearly 80 percent of the automobile loan sources identified and about the same percentage of cash loan sources. In financing a home, banks were identified as the likely source by 45 percent of the families and savings and loan firms by 17 percent.

In structuring a marketing program aimed at mobiles, banks should be keenly aware of the limited time available to contact mobiles after a move. Specific programs need to be undertaken to contact mobiles prior to arrival, if possible, or within a week of their move into a new community. Prior contact of newcomers might profitably be made by mail to individuals planning a move into the community. Knowledge of transfers or new appointments would be essential. Recommendations, convenience, and prior experience all play major roles in the bank selection process. Marketing messages aimed at newcomers should be structured to reflect the factors influencing the selection of a bank. Banks should stress the availability of loans when contacting mobiles. Mobiles moving into the market area of a bank should receive by mail detailed literature offering specific banking services. If mobiles are not contacted the first week of arrival the opportunities of a bank receiving a new account would appear to be relatively limited and dependent upon convenience and recommendations.

Promotional messages should be aimed at husbands because they play such a vital role in the bank selection process. As in the selection of property insurance, individuals concerned with property transfers play a major role in influencing bank selections. A promotional program aimed at newcomers should be reflective of the key segments of the population likely to influence bank selection decisions.

Savings and loan firms are selected primarily to finance homes and their advertising should reflect the use made of the funds. Competition between various financial institutions should be considered in structuring a promotional program for any one. Mobiles take from two to four weeks on the average to select savings and loan firms. Thus promotion by these firms to the mobile market segment might be delayed until knowledge was gained of the new addresses, at home and work, of the husband. Credit unions typically have a market limited to employees of a specific firm or organization. Promotion to the market by credit unions should be tied in with contacts made to the household head at the place of employment as well as at home.

It would appear that banks which do not attract mobiles shortly after arrival have another opportunity to reach the market when a decision is made to open a savings account. Promotion to the market segment can also be made at the somewhat later date when savings accounts are typically opened. Promotions should feature earnings on savings, convenience, or hours of service, rather than features used to initially attract new families. Successful promotion in the area may be a way to counter poor locations, or the influence of recommendations both which may hinder the initial efforts of some banks to gain new customers.

Insurance

Research findings reveal that mobile families are more likely to purchase property insurance than either automobile insurance or life insurance. New property insurance was purchased by 45 percent of the families after moving. Less than 20 percent purchased automobile insurance and about 15 percent purchased life insurance. Property insurance was usually purchased after families had been in the community over three weeks, although in some cases it was purchased by the husband prior to the arrival of the family. Automobile insurance purchases were made on the average five weeks after arrival. Life insurance purchases typically were made after a family had resided in the community longer than seven weeks.

Families tended to select property insurance suppliers after a visit to only one firm. Life insurance purchases also were generally made after contacting only one potential supplier, although a number of families visited two firms. The greatest amount of comparison shopping in selecting insurance suppliers was found in the area of automobile insurance, where purchases were typically made after the families had contacted two suppliers

The decision responsibility for selecting insurance suppliers rested primarily with the husband. Husbands played the major role in nearly three-quarters of all the purchase selections. Husbands alone usually made the decisions in the area of property insurance; however, in the automobile and life insurance areas joint decisions with their wives were made in about 20 percent of the purchases. In learning about various suppliers of insurance, mobile families relied almost exclusively upon personal information. For example, in selecting property insurance, mobile families frequently received recommendations from builders, lawyers, bankers, or realtors. Mobile families generally were unable to identify names of property insurance companies carrying the family insurance. However, they were generally able to identify the agency or person from which the insurance was purchased. In the automobile and life insurance areas mobile families tended to identify the insurance company rather than an agent or agency. In selecting life insurance, personal contacts were made by sales personnel who played a major role in providing families with information on potential suppliers.

Although automobile and life insurance had been purchased by less than one-quarter of the families, the families were able to identify favorite companies in over two-thirds of the interviews. Generally the favorite companies identified were the firms currently supplying policies to the families.

Each family in the sample was asked to give reasons for selecting specific companies as favorites. Nearly one-third of the families gave "carry insurance with the firm now" or "previous experience with the firm" as the major reasons; "low rates" were also frequently indicated. Recommendations of friends or relatives or having a friend selling for a specific company were also important reasons given for selecting insurance suppliers.

In planning a program aimed at mobile consumers it might be a good idea for insurance companies to concentrate on contacting their customers who move from one company sales district to another. This continued contact with mobiles is of particular importance to automobile and life insurance firms. While less than 20 percent of the mobile families in this study purchased new insurance, they continued the life and automobile policies they had. To maintain market position with mobiles, life and automobile insurance firms should maintain data on the changes in residence of policy holders and transmit such data between offices.

Property insurance firms and representatives should follow a slightly different market strategy. The prime concern of firms in the property insurance field should be to develop a continual source of knowledge on property transfers to mobiles. Bankers, lawyers, and real estate people typically have major roles in influencing purchase decisions in the sale of property insurance. Since purchasers tend to identify agencies rather than firms, each agency should stress programs aimed at the mobile market segment featuring the agency name and lines of insurance sold.

In contacting possible property insurance purchasers agencies should contact mobiles immediately upon arrival. Contact should be made with the head of the household. Life and automobile insurance contacts could be made shortly after a family arrives and prior to the completion of six weeks in the community. It is important to consider the wives when contacting mobile families for new automobile and life policies because of the high family income levels and density of women drivers. Familiarity of the insuring company would appear to be the major element to be stressed in developing programs used in contacting mobiles for purchases of life and automobile insurance.

Furniture and Appliances

The mobile families interviewed had spent $91,615.00 for furniture and appliances within four months after completing their long distance moves. The expenditures averaged $623.33 for each of the 147 families in the sample. The rate of expenditure was nearly twice the $314.00 yearly expenditure for all families in the nation.[9]

Mobile families typically bought 40 percent of their furniture and appliances during the first month of residence in the community. About 25 percent of all expenditures were made during the second month, 20 percent the third month, and the remaining 15 percent during the fourth month of residence.

Mobile families generally purchased appliances before furniture. Families making purchases from two different appliance suppliers selected the first store during their first week in the community and the second store, on the average, during the third week. Furniture purchases were typically made after living in the community six or seven weeks. Considerably more shopping was done in the selection of furniture stores than appliance stores. For example, the first appliance store was generally selected after a visit to only one other store. However, two furniture stores were usually visited before making the contact which resulted in the initial furniture purchase.

Wives played the key role in selecting furniture stores. They made the selection of furniture stores alone nearly half the time and participated jointly with their husbands in an almost equal amount of decisions. The selection of appliance stores was generally found to be an undertaking of both the husband and wife. Nearly half the decisions were in the joint category. Husbands alone made the supplier selection decisions in nearly 13 percent of all families. Thus husbands and wives jointly appeared to play the major role in the selection of appliance stores while wives alone assumed the chief responsibility in selecting furniture stores. Each mobile family was asked to indicate the person in the family who selected the brand of furniture and appliances. Responses revealed that the responsibility for selecting brands was generally assumed by the person or persons selecting the suppliers.

Mobile families concentrated one-third of all their furniture and appliance purchases with the local outlet of one national organization. The largest local independently owned department store was able to attract slightly over 13 percent of the purchases made by the mobile group. No other retailer attained over 4 percent of these purchases. One hundred and eight purchases were made with twenty-three local firms, for an averave of 4.7 sales per firm. The eight regionally operated firms were able to attract twenty purchases, or an average of 2.5 sales, per firm. The five national organizations made ninety-three sales to mobiles or an average of 18.6 sales per firm.

Reasons given by mobiles for selecting suppliers fell into two major categories: range of selection of items carried, and brand preference or previous experience with a firm. The second factor supported the market position of the national organization which received the largest share of the furniture and appliance business. Slightly over one-half of all furniture and appliance items purchased were bought using credit. The strong market position of the one firm can be further explained by the fact that nearly 50 percent of the mobile families were able to transfer an account to the local outlet of the organization.

Style was selected first in nearly two-thirds of the purchases of furniture. The store was selected first in 20 percent of the purchases. Brand and store were selected first almost equally in choosing appliance suppliers. Style was not mentioned as a major factor in the selection of appliances. Appliances most frequently purchased by mobiles were washers, dryers, refrigerators, and stoves. In the furniture area, purchases were concentrated in the living room. Couches and chairs accounted for 20.5 percent of all purchases; draperies and lamps, 25.2 percent.

Designing a marketing strategy for mobile consumers is especially important for locally owned retailers of furniture and appliances. Mobiles comprise a unique market segment with a purchase rate twice the national average. In this study the outlet of one national chain enjoyed one-third of all the furniture and appliance purchases made by mobiles. It would appear that charge account transfers, brand loyalty, and store familiarity all tend to make the selection process easy for many mobile consumers; mobiles patronize familiar chain outlets in their shopping soon after arrival.

The dominance of purchases from one firm in the market area studied makes it appear that chain outlets have an important initial advantage over locally owned stores, regardless of the local firm's size. The advantage is probably because of the lack of information mobiles have on local suppliers.

Promotional programs in the furniture and appliance area would appear to be especially necessary for the local organizations which do not have the familiarity enjoyed by multi-unit retailers. For furniture, the promotional programs should be aimed primarily at the wives; for appliances, at both husband and wife. Because of the heavy use made of credit in durable goods purchases, efforts should be made by local retailers to add long distance mobiles to store credit lists immediately after their arrival. Direct mail and personal contacts are effective ways to reach the market. Advertisements in the yellow pages should specify the brands of merchandise carried.

Promotional programs by furniture stores may be initiated somewhat later than the programs of stores selling appliances only. Appliance purchases are made soon after arrival, but furniture purchases are typically made from six to ten weeks after a family has been in the community. Promotions directed to the mobile market segment should feature items most frequently purchased by mobiles: washers, dryers, refrigerators, and stoves in the appliance area; emphasis should be on living room furnishings in the furniture area. Furniture promotions should feature the style of merchandise offered. While the relative affluence of the mobile market segment has been established, the families leading in this study frequently listed price or item on sale as prime factors in the selection of suppliers. Purchases of items on sale, to the mobile market segment, were frequently aided by the use of mass media. Perhaps the most direct way a local furniture or appliance retailer could attract mobiles would be to send them a letter introducing the firm, asking for patronage, and enclosing a credit application. Firms at which mobiles already have accounts should make the rapid flow of information on changes in address a regular operating procedure. Thus, the outlet in the new area can invite the mobile family into the store to carry on the present mutual association.

Men's Suits and Women's Better Dresses and Suits

Slightly more than one-quarter of the families purchased either a man's suit or a woman's better dress within four months after their arrival. About half of these purchases were made by using a charge account. Newcomers selected the store first in nearly 80 percent of the purchases; the brand of merchandise was selected first in the other 20 percent of purchases.

Women's clothing, of the type studied, was purchased on the average seven weeks after a family moved into the area; men's suits were purchased after eight weeks. In selecting a supplier for the initial local purchase of a man's suit, mobiles usually visited two shops and then made their purchase in the second shop. It took three shop visits to select women's dresses. Wives chose the suppliers of women's clothing in virtually all of the mobile families. Selection of suppliers for men's suits was mostly done by the husbands, although women helped in some 20 percent of the selections. Mobiles relied on personal information in nearly two-thirds of the purchases. Recommendations of friends and co-workers were of prime importance in selecting clothing suppliers for both men and women.

Reasons most frequently given for selecting suppliers were, "liked what they had," good selection, and price. Families who had not purchased clothing of the type studied in the community prior to their interview, were asked to identify how clothing suppliers would be selected. Factors most mentioned were: shop around for a store (42.9 percent), ask others (40.9 percent), and read newspaper advertisements (10.2 percent).

The first consideration in proposing a marketing strategy for clothing merchants is the size and nature of the market. Evidence from the sample seems to indicate that mobiles, at least in the first months of residence in a community, do not typically purchase a man's suit or a woman's better dress or suit. The time between arrival and purchase pinpoints the need to plan contacts with mobiles after the newcomers have been in the community a period of time. Such contacts can be directed at either the husband or wife, depending upon the nature of the item. Direct mail contacts inviting mobiles to open charge accounts and stressing brands of merchandise would appear to be an excellent way to contact newcomers.

While research showed that personal recommendations played a key role in the selection of clothing stores, advertisements in newspapers frequently created the desire to buy from one firm. Mobiles mentioned that advertisements emphasizing price were particularly valuable. A marketing strategy for mobiles should certainly reflect price considerations as well as attention to transfer customers. In the case of smaller specialty stores a promotional program with a local welcoming organization would appear to be an excellent way to introduce a store to newcomers. Since in the clothing area newcomers are prone to make purchases based upon personal recommendations, the use of a welcoming service appears to be useful. Such a contact could introduce the brands of merchandise carried, offer the newcomer a gift certificate for an item of clothing which can be picked up at the store, and include a charge account application.

Medical Service

Table 5-1 reflects the use of medical services by mobile families. During the first four months in the community, nearly one-half of the families used at least one medical service. Less than 50 percent of the families selected individuals to perform medical services before they actually needed medical attention.

TABLE 5-1
Use of Medical Services

Medical Services	Used Number	Used Percent	Not Used Number	Not Used Percent	Total Number	Total Percent
General practitioners	78	53.3	69	46.7	147	100.0
Specialists	74	50.3	73	49.7	147	100.0
Dentists	70	47.6	77	52.4	147	100.0

Mobiles tended to select specialists, on the average, 6.9 weeks after arrival. General practitioners were selected during the seventh week and dentists after nine weeks in the community. In no case did the families in this study visit more than one potential supplier in making a choice. The responsibility for selecting medical services resided primarily with the wives. Wives alone made the decisions on which medical services to use in nearly half of the families. Wives participated jointly with husbands in making decisions in another one third of the families. Husbands alone played only a minor role in decisions on selecting medical services.

Families learned of the medical sources used, in practically all cases, through personal information. Medical suppliers were selected by sixty-eight families based upon non-professional sources. The breakdown of sources used is contained in Table 5-2. A comparison of nonprofessional sources to receivers revealed that nonprofessional sources were always married and were nearly always of the same sex as the receivers. In one-half the cases those who provided the information were the same age as the receivers, earned about the same income and had the

TABLE 5-2

Distribution of Medical Services Selected
Based on Nonprofessional Sources

Type of Medical Service Selected	Number of Families	
	Number	Percent
General practitioner	24	35.3
General practitioner and specialist	4	5.9
General practitioner and dentist	7	10.3
Specialist	9	13.2
Specialist and dentist	7	10.3
Dentist	12	17.7
General practitioner, specialist, and dentist	5	7.3
TOTAL	68	100.0

same number of children. A third of the time individuals providing medical data were older, enjoyed a better income, and
had more children than the receivers.

An analysis of reasons given for selecting specific medical
services reveals that recommendations of professional sources
played a key role in one-fifth of all selections. However, recommendations of nonprofessionals (22.8 percent) were of slightly
greater importance. In some 11 percent of the families, convenience played the deciding role. A willingness on behalf of a
doctor or dentist to accept new patients and make house calls
was the reason given for selection by nearly 17 percent. Almost
90 percent of the families studied were satisfied with the initial
medical service.

Promotion efforts of the medical and dental professions are
rigidly controlled by ethics. However, certain professional practices had a major role in the process by which mobiles selected
suppliers. Mobile families tended to rely almost exclusively
upon personal information sources when selecting medical services. Professional references appear to be vital to a doctor or
dentist hoping to service patients in the mobile market area.

The willingness to take new patients and make house calls
played key roles in the selection process; convenience was also
of importance. The logical way for the medical and dental pro-
fession to serve mobiles would be to provide public knowledge

on which professional individuals would be willing to assume new patients. Another means used by mobiles to select medical service personnel was to read the introductory notices as new offices were opened. Mobiles tended to view such newcomers as being like themselves and expected to be able to receive appointments with the new personnel. Thus, medical and dental personnel would serve the mobile market segment primarily by making known the willingness to take new patients.

How the Average Family Rebuilt Sources of Supply in Ten Weeks After Moving

Immediately upon arrival in a new community the mobile family selected the first food supplier. This selection was made by the wife after a brief search of the trading area immediately surrounding her new residence. Within the first week or two the husband made the selection of a bank to handle the family checking account. The bank selected was close to home and was chosen after talking to a number of individuals in the community.

In the third week after arrival the wife selected the favorite supermarket. The selection was made after visits to two or three possible suppliers. Selection of the first supermarket was based upon convenience, but the favorite store was selected because of the quality of its meat or produce. The first appliance purchase was made sometime during the third week after moving into the community. Selection of the supplier was made jointly by the husband and wife after searching through two possible suppliers. A savings and loan firm was also selected three weeks after arrival. The selection was made by the husband based upon personal information obtained from an individual associated with the transfer of property to the family. Three weeks after arrival the purchase of property insurance was made by the husband. The firm or agency providing the insurance was learned about by the husband through personal contacts with people in the community.

In the fourth week after arrival the first dry cleaning was

done for the family. The dry cleaning was done in a conventional operation and was taken to the firm performing the service. The family used a coupon given by a welcoming service to have the first cleaning done. The coupon was the prime reason for selecting the first firm used by the family. The wife selected the first cleaner. The credit union was the third financial institution used by the family and it was selected four weeks after arrival. The credit union joined was learned about through the husband's employer and was used to secure a short term loan for family needs.

During the fifth week after arrival the wife selected her first beauty parlor using a coupon received from a welcoming organization. Another purchase made during the fifth week after arrival was that of an automobile insurance policy. The selection was made by the husband after contacting two firms. The firm selling insurance to the family usually contacted the family and asked for the business. The second major appliance purchase was also made during the fifth week. The second purchase was made after visits to three possible suppliers. The firm was selected jointly by the husband and wife after a search of the trading area.

Six weeks after arrival the housewife selected her favorite beauty parlor. The selection was made after visits to two local beauty parlors. Typically, the favorite was not the first shop used because of the poor appearance of the first shop or its operators. During the sixth week the wife also selected the favorite family dry cleaner. The cleaner she selected did the work in a conventional manner and was chosen after two or three firms had been tried. The cleaner chosen was close to home. Furniture was purchased in two stores during the sixth week of residence in the community. Furniture store selections were made by the wife alone or jointly with her husband. Personal information and searching were used to get information about furniture suppliers. Furniture purchases required visits to two or three possible suppliers and they were made by using a charge account transferred from another community.

In the seventh week after arrival the wife purchased a better dress or suit. The selection entailed visits to three clothing suppliers and was made primarily through information gained from talking to other women. Searching through the stores also provided information on clothing suppliers. The mobile family needed to select a general practitioner and specialist during the seventh week. Selections were made by the wife with some help from the husband. The specialist was selected earlier in the week, before the general practitioner. Selections of both doctors were based upon the recommendations received from other individuals. The source of information was more often nonprofessional than professional.

In the eighth week after arrival the husband purchased his first suit from a local firm. His selection was made after visits to a number of stores. Personal information received from friends and searching provided aid in the shopping process. The wife was of some help in the selection of the first men's clothing store. The third furniture store was also selected during the eighth week of residence. The selection of the third furniture store was an undertaking of both the husband and wife and entailed visits to three or four possible suppliers. During the eighth week the family purchased a life insurance policy. The selection was made by the husband after talking to friends and insurance representatives.

In the ninth week after arrival the family selected a dentist. The selection was made by the wife and was based upon information received from friends.

A Particularly Important Market for Suppliers

The long distance mobile market is especially critical to the one unit or multi-unit locally operated retail organization. The overall concept of mobility means the population in an average area would completely change in a five year period. One unit retailers need to continually adjust the marketing program used to reflect changes in the market. Promotion to the special mobile market segment would appear to be much more important for the single unit unknown retailer than for the relatively well-known multi-unit operations. For the single unit operation mobility makes a continual introductory program for newcomers vital.

Multi-unit operators face a slightly different problem in marketing to mobiles. The problem for multi-unit operations is how to insure that customers faithfully patronizing an outlet before moving will transfer patronage to the chain outlet near their new place of residence. In light of the varying nature of competition in different markets, the strategy used by a chain in one market to gain consumer franchise may not be the appropriate strategy to use in another area. The benefits of similar identification of centrally owned outlets would appear to make uniform store identification an increasingly important concept for retailing in the future. The need to attain some familiarity or similarity of merchandising operations would also seem apparent. The chain operation desiring to attract mobiles must balance efforts geared to one particular geographic market with efforts geared to the mass market in several different geographic areas.

This research established that families once identified as mobiles are likely to move again. Some family units may spend an appreciable part of the family life cycle in the mobile market segment. Continual transfers of mobiles would appear to be an expected characteristic of society in the future. Consumer ties to one particular retailer in the case of local firms, will be increasingly dependent on the brands of merchandise and price lines offered. National or regional chains will have an advantage, at least initially, in gaining the business of mobiles in each market.

The mobile market is a key area of market opportunity for firms primarily associated with uprooting, moving, and settling mobile families in new places of residence. Firms such as moving companies, real estate companies, financial institutions and insurance companies, could well gear all or part of the firm's promotional strategy to the mobile market. Moving companies could well afford to maintain continual contact with families once a move has been completed; the same family is a prime prospect for another move. In the same sense insurance firms should be sure that marketing programs include provisions for contacting mobiles immediately upon completion of the move to make sure that needed changes in existing policies are made. Financial institutions, particularly banks, are typically associated with mobiles before and after a change in residence. The home loan market for mobile families would appear to be an important market opportunity for financial institutions. Financial institutions can be expected to play key roles in the transfer of property from one family to another family, possibly another mobile. Contacting mobiles soon after arrival could be a possible way to increase both private and professional business by gaining accounts from newcomers in the community, because of the nature of the occupations of mobile household heads.

Tactics to Be Used in Programs
Aimed at Mobiles

If management anticipates specific benefits from marketing to mobiles several decisions must be made after a firm evaluates its total marketing effort. These decisions are the same regardless of the size of the firm.

Assuming the market potential is able to support a special mobile marketing program, the first step would be to obtain an immediate and accurate source of names of mobiles. Then consideration must be given to how the market should be contacted. Decisions need to be made on which families should be contacted, how they should be contacted, when they should be contacted, and if a particular family member should be contacted. In this area the services of a welcoming service might be employed.

Following the solution of the tactical questions attention needs to be turned to the nature of the promotional program to be used. Should coupons or gifts be used? Should the program be tied to the opening of a charge account? Included in the promotional decision area should be questions on the implementation of such a program as part of the overall program of the firm. Coordination and evaluation should be major guidelines in structuring a marketing strategy for the mobile market. The mobile program must be coordinated in the total marketing plan of the firm and subject to consistant evaluation. Because of the distinct character of the mobile market even relatively small firms can judge the impact of programs aimed at mobiles. Such an evaluation can be made simply by checking on the sales of the firm to newcomers contacted particularly if such sales are made using credit or invoice. A possible danger of overall evaluation should be noted. If a firm is generally unable to pinpoint the effectiveness of the total promotional expenditure, care should be taken to insure that overly precise expectations of revenues from a program directed at mobiles do not lead to their termination. Another guide line would be to confine the program aimed at mobiles to a firm's regular marketing area, especially in the early stages of a program.

In particular, programs geared to mobiles should be timed to reach them before judgments have been made on suppliers in the family's new trading area. Special attention should also be devoted to contacting the proper person or persons, as well as using the most appropriate media in terms of the program limitations and objectives.

Impact of Mobility in the Future

The long distance mobile segment is expected to comprise over fifteen million individuals by 1975. While the average rate of mobility is a valuable guide to the overall concept of mobility, specific areas have in the past and are in the future expected to have mobility rates far in the excess of the one-move-every-five-year national figure. In particular, the West and Southwestern states are expected to continue the rapid turnover of population. The most interesting concept concerning mobility may be the unique patterns of mobility within specific middle and upper middle class neighborhoods within metropolitan areas. The suburban areas, populated by individuals with high aspirations of mobility and employed by multi-location organizations may be expected to have rates of mobility far above the national average.

This research has dealt with the relatively young, well-educated, middle and upper middle class white collar worker. The market segment investigated was composed of people who were typically prone to repeated mobility. To marketers, the identification of where such individuals reside adds yet another dimension to the overall concept of mobility. Specific address or city areas may even be designated for promotional campaigns designed to capture a share of this affluent mobile market.

The presence of mobility as a phenomenon of the market place of the coming decades seems assured. The challenge to marketers will be to successfully design programs useful in gaining the patronage of families in the market segment identified and described in this research.

Notes

Chapter I

1. U. S. Bureau of the Census, *Current Population Reports, Series P-20, No. 156, Mobility of the Population of the United States: March, 1965 to March, 1966* (Washington, D. C.: U. S. Government Printing Office, 1966), p. 1.

2. "Consumer Dynamics—Part II: The Movers," *Progressive Grocer* (November, 1965), pp. K 37, K 38.

3. "Consumer Dynamics," *op. cit.*, pp. K 37, K 38.

4. *Ibid.*

5. The combined supplier selection pattern is composed of four elements: (1) information sources used by families in selecting suppliers, (2) the individuals making the purchase decision in each category, (3) the time taken by mobile families to select new suppliers upon completion of a move, and (4) the number of potential suppliers visited before a supplier is selected within a purchase category.

6. Alan R. Andreasen, "Geographic Mobility and Market Segmentation," *Journal of Marketing Research*, III (November, 1966), pp. 341-45.

7. L. R. Klein and J. B. Lansing, "Decisions to Purchase Consumer Durable Goods," *The Journal of Marketing*, XX (October, 1955), p. 111.

8. "Consumer Dynamics," *op. cit.*, pp. K 38-K 39.

Chapter II

1. Fred J. Borch, "The Marketing Philosophy as a Way of Business Life," *Managerial Marketing: Perspectives and Viewpoints*, ed. William Lazer and Eugene J. Kelley (Homewood, Ill.: Richard D. Irwin, Inc., 1962), p. 15.

89

2. James U. McNeal, "Consumer Behavior—Introduction," *Dimensions of Consumer Behavior*, ed. James U. McNeal (New York: Appleton-Century Crofts, 1965), p. 7.

3. Thomas A. Staudt, "The Managerial Functions of Marketing," ed. William Lazer and Eugene J. Kelley, *Managerial Marketing: Perspectives and Viewpoints* (Homewood, Ill.: Richard D. Irwin, Inc., 1962), pp. 386-87.

4. McNeal, *op. cit.*, p. 301.

5. Wendall R. Smith, "Product Differentiation and Market Segmentation as Alternative Marketing Strategies," *Journal of Marketing*, XXI (July, 1956), pp. 3-8.

6. Milton Alexander, "The Significance of Ethnic Groups in Marketing Type Packaged Foods in Greater New York," *Advancing Marketing Efficiency*, ed. Lynn H. Stockman (Chicago: American Marketing Association, 1959), pp. 557-61.

7. Peggy Boomer, "Male Market: Big-Rich-But-Tough," *Printers Ink*, CCLXXX (July 20, 1962), pp. 21-25.

8. David E. Wollin, "A Marketing Profile of the Senior Citizen Group," *Marketing's Role in Scientific Management*, ed. Robert L. Clewett (Chicago: American Marketing Association, 1957), pp. 250-61.

9. Paul E. Smith, "Merchandising for the Teen-Age Market," *Journal of Retailing*, XXXVII (Summer, 1961), pp. 9-13.

10. Robert Ferber, "Our Changing Consumer Market," *Business Horizons*, I (Spring, 1958), pp. 49-66.

11. James Gillies, "The Population Explosion—Its Implications for Business," *California Management Review*, III (Winter, 1961), pp. 53-60.

12. "The Working Man: Do Marketing Men Know Him?" *Printers Ink*, CCLXXVII (December 1, 1961), pp. 48- 49.

13. Pierre Martineau, "Social Class and Spending Behavior," *Journal of Marketing*, XXIII (October, 1958), pp. 121-30.

14. Morris J. Gottlieb, "Segmentation by Personality Types," *Advancing Marketing Efficiency*, ed. Lynn Stockman (Chicago: American Marketing Association, 1959), pp. 148-58.

15. Edward L. Grubb, "Consumer Perception of Self Concept: Its Relation to Brand Choice of Selected Product Types," *Marketing and Economic Development*, ed. Peter D. Bennett (Chicago: American Marketing Association, 1965), pp. 419-22.

16. William E. Bell, "Consumer Innovation: An Investigation of Selected Characteristics of Innovators" (DBA dissertation, College of Business Administration, Michigan State University, 1962), p. 293.

17. James M. Carman, *The Application of Social Class in Market Segmentation* (Berkeley: Institute of Business and Economic Research, University of California, 1965), p. 60.

18. U. S. Bureau of the Census, *Current Population Reports, Series P-20, No.. 156, Mobility of the Population of the United States: March, 1965 to March, 1966* (Washington, D. C.: U. S. Government Printing Office, 1966), pp. 1-4.

19. *Ibid.*

20. *Ibid.*

21. *Ibid.,* pp. 2-3.

22. *Ibid.*

23. U. S. Bureau of the Census, *Current Population Reports, Series P-20, No. 154, Reasons for Moving: March, 1962 to March, 1963* (Washington, D. C.: U. S. Government Printing Office, 1966), p. 1.

24. Andreasen, "Geographic Mobility and Market Segmentation," *op. cit.,* p. 342.

25. Alfred R. Oxenfeldt, "Consumer Knowledge: Its Measurement and Extent," *Review of Economics and Statistics,* XXXII (November, 1960), pp. 300-14.

26. Sidney P. Feldman and Merlin C. Spencer, "The Effect of Personal Influence in the Selection of Consumer Services," *Marketing and Economic Development,* ed. Peter D. Bennett (Chicago: American Marketing Association, 1965), pp. 440-48.

27. The Foundation for Research on Human Behavior, *Adoption of New Products* (Ann Arbor: University of Michigan, 1959), p. 9.

28. George J. Stigler, "The Economics of Information," *Journal of Political Economy,* LXIX (June, 1961), p. 213.

29. John B. Roberts, *Sources of Information and Food Buying Decisions,* Southern Cooperative Series Bulletin No. 85 (Lexington: University of Kentucky Agriculture Station, April, 1963), p. 50.

30. James H. Meyers, "A Competitive Edge in Marketing Communication," *Competition in Marketing,* ed. Taylor W. Meloan and Charles M. Whitle (University of Southern California, 1964), p. 82.

31. George Katona, *The Powerful Consumer* (New York: McGraw Hill Book Company, Inc., 1960), p. 157.

32. George Katona and Eva Mueller, "A Study of Purchase Decisions," *Consumer Behavior: Vol. I: The Dynamics of Consumer Reaction,* ed. Lincoln Clark (New York: New York University Press, 1954), p. 112.

33. Elihu Katz and Paul F. Lazarsfeld, *Personal Influence* (Glencoe Ill.: The Free Press, 1955), p. 234.

34. William H. Whyte, Jr., "The Web of Word of Mouth," *Fortune*, L (November, 1964), p. 208.

35. Francis S. Bourne, "Group Influence in Marketing and Public Relations," *Marketing in Progress*, ed. H. C. Barksdale (New York: Holt, Rhinehart and Winston, 1964), p. 332.

36. Frederick E. May, "Buying Behavior: Some Research Findings," *Journal of Business*, XXXVII (October, 1965), p. 384.

37. James Morgan, "A Review of Recent Research on Consumer Behavior," *Consumer Behavior: Research on Consumer Reaction*, ed. Lincoln H. Clark (New York: Harper and Brothers), 1958, p. 144.

38. George Katona and Eva Mueller, "A Study of Purchase Decisions," *Consumer Behavior: Vol. I: The Dynamics of Consumer Reaction, op. cit.* p. 80.

39. Harry Sharp and Paul Mott, "Consumer Decisions in the Metropolitan Family," *Journal of Marketing*, XXI (October 1956), p. 155.

40. William F. Kenkel, "Decision Making and the Life Cycle— Husband-Wife Interaction in Decision Making and Decision Choices," *Journal of Applied Psychology*, LIV (November, 1961), pp. 255-60.

41. Feldman and Spencer, *op. cit.*, p. 450.

42. Henry O. Whiteside, "Interacting Roles of the Household Purchasing Agent," in *Theory in Marketing*, ed. Reavis Cox, Wroe Alderson and Stanley J. Shapiro (Homewood, Ill.: Richard D. Irwin, Inc., 1964), p. 270.

43. Alan R. Andreasen, "Attitudes and Customer Behavior: A Decision Model," *New Research in Marketing*, ed. Lee E. Preston (Berkeley: Institute of Business and Economic Research, University of California, 1965), pp. 2-16.

44. Pierre Martineau, "Social Classes and Spending Behavior," *Journal of Marketing*, XXIII (October, 1958), p. 126.

45. Bruce Legrand and John G. Udell, "Consumer Behavior in the Market Place," *Journal of Retailing*, LX (Fall, 1964), p. 32.

46. Wesley C. Bender, "Consumer Purchase Costs—Do Retailers Recognize Them," *Journal of Retailing* (Spring, 1964), pp. 1-8.

47. Louis P. Bucklin, "Retail Strategy and the Classification of Consumer Goods," *Journal of Marketing*, XXVII (January, 1963), p. 53.

48. Richard N. Cardozo, "An Experimental Study of Consumer Effort, Expectation and Satisfaction," *Journal of Marketing Research*, II (August, 1965), p. 248.

49. Perry Bliss, "Supply Considerations and Shopper Convenience," *Journal of Marketing* (July, 1966), pp. 43-45.

50. Donald F. Blankertz, "Motivation and Rationalization in Retail Buying," *Public Opinion Quarterly*, XII (Winter, 1949), pp. 659-68.

51. Janet L. Wolff, *What Makes Women Buy* (New York: McGraw-Hill Book Company, 1958), p. 46.

52. Kenward L. Atkin, "Communications Patterns and Effect in Super Market Choice" (Ph.D. dissertation, Michigan State University, 1961), p. 315.

53. "Consumer Dynamics," *op. cit.*, pp. 49-50.

54. *Ibid.*

Chapter V

1. U. S. Bureau of the Census, Statistical Abstract of the United States; 1966 (87th edition) (Washington, D. C.: U. S. Government Printing Office, 1966), p. 113.

2. *Ibid.*, p. 336.

3. Sales Management Survey of Buying Power, *Sales Management*, XCVI (June 10, 1966), p. B 3.

4. Statistical Abstract of the United States: 1966, *op. cit.*, p. 229.

5. Andreasen, "Geographic Mobility and Market Segmentation," *op. cit.*, pp. 340-41.

6. *Ibid.*

7. *Ibid.*

8. E. Jerome McCarthy, *Basic Marketing: A Managerial Approach* (Homewood, Ill., Richard D. Irwin, Inc., 1964), pp. 21-46.

9. Fabian Linden (ed.), *Expenditure Patterns of the American Family* (New York: National Industrial Conference Board, 1965), pp. 70-77.

Bibliography

Public Documents

Adoption of New Products, The Foundation for Research on Human Behavior, Ann Arbor: University of Michigan, 1959.

Linden, Fabian, ed. *Expenditure Patterns of the American Family.* New York: National Industrial Conference Board, 1965.

Roberts, John B. *Sources of Information and Food Buying Decisions.* Southern Cooperative Series Bulletin No. 85, University of Kentucky Agriculture Station, 1963.

Survey of Super Market Shoppers. Cincinnati: Burgoyne Index, Inc. 1962.

U. S. Bureau of the Census. *Current Population Reports, Series P-20, No. 154, "Reasons for Moving: March 1962 to March 1963."* Washington: U. S. Government Printing Office, 1966.

U. S. Bureau of the Census. *Current Population Reports, Series P-20, No. 156, "Mobility of the Population of the United States: March 1965 to March 1966."* Washington: U. S. Government Printing Office, 1966.

U. S. Bureau of the Census. *U. S. Census of Population: 1960, Vol. 1, Characteristics of the Population. Part 24, Michigan.* Washington: U. S. Government Printing Office, 1963.

U. S. Bureau of the Census. *Statistical Abstract of the United States,* Washington: U. S. Government Printing Office, 1966.

Books

Berlo, David K. *The Process of Communication.* New York: Holt, Rinehart and Winston, 1961.

Foote, Wilson N., ed. *Household Decision Making.* New York: New York University Press, 1961.

Hamilton, David. *The Consumer in Our Economy.* Cambridge: The Riverside Press, 1962.

Katona, George. *The Powerful Consumer.* New York: McGraw Hill Book Company, Inc., 1960.

Katz, Elihu and Lazarsfeld, Paul F. *Personal Influence.* Glencoe: The Free Press, 1965.

Lazer, William and Kelley, Eugene, ed. *Managerial Marketing: Perspectives and Viewpoints.* Homewood, Ill.: Richard D. Irwin, Inc., 1964.

McCarthy, E. Jerome. *Basic Marketing A Managerial Approach.* Homewood: Richard D. Irwin, Inc., 1964.

McNeal, James, ed. *Dimensions of Consumer Behavior.* New York: Appleton-Century Crofts, 1965.

Rainwater, Lee, Coleman, Richard P. and Handel, Gerald. *Working Man's Wife.* New York: Oceana Publications, Inc., 1959.

Reiss, Albert J., Jr. *Occupations and Social Status.* Glencoe: The Free Press, 1961.

Wolff, Janet L. *What Makes Women Buy.* New York: McGraw-Hill Book Company, 1958.

Articles and Periodicals

Alderson and Sessions. "Basic Research Report on Consumer Behavior: Report on a Study of Shopping Behavior and Methods for Its Investigation," *Research Design in Marketing,* ed. Ronald E. Frank. Homewood, Ill.: Richard D. Irwin, Inc., 1962, pp. 129-45.

Alexander, Milton. "The Significance of Ethnic Groups in Marketing New-Type Package Foods in Greater New York," *Advancing Marketing Efficiency,* ed. Lynn H. Stockman. Chicago: American Marketing Association, 1959, pp. 557-61.

Andreasen, Alan R. "Attitudes and Customer Behavior: A Decision Model," *New Research in Marketing,* ed. Lee E. Preston. Berkeley: Institute of Business and Economic Research, University of California, 1965, pp. 1-17.

――――――――――. "Geographic Mobility and Market Segmentation," *Journal of Marketing Research,* III (Nov. 1966), pp. 341-48.

Bender, Wesley. "Consumer Purchase Costs—Do Retailers Recognize Them," *Journal of Retailing,* XL (Spring, 1964), pp. 1-8, 52.

Blankertz, Donald F. "Motivation and Rationalization in Retail Buying," *Public Opinion Quarterly,* XIII (Winter, 1949), pp. 659-68.

Bliss, Perry. "Supply Considerations and Shopper Convenience," *Journal of Marketing,* XXV (July, 1966), pp. 43-45.

Boomer, Peggy. "Male Market: Big-Rich-But-Tough," *Printers Ink,* CCLXXX (July, 1962), pp. 21-25.

Borch, Fred J. "The Marketing Philosophy as a Way of Business Life," *Managerial Marketing: Prospectives and Viewpoints*, ed. William Lazer and Eugene Kelley. Homewood, Ill.: Richard D. Irwin, Inc., 1962, pp. 14-20.

Bourne, Francis S. "Group Influence in Marketing and Public Relations," *Marketing in Progress*, ed. H. C. Barksdale. New York: Holt, Rinehart and Winston (1964), pp. 332-56.

Bucklin, Louis P. "Retail Strategy and the Classification of Consumer Goods," *Journal of Marketing*, XXVII (January, 1963), pp. 50-55.

Cardozo, Richard N. "An Experimental Study of Consumer Effort, Expectation and Satisfaction," *Journal of Marketing Research*, II (August, 1965), pp. 244-49.

"Consumer Dynamics—Part II: The Movers," *Progressive Grocer*, XLIV (November, 1965), K35-K58.

Cunningham, Ross M. "Customer Loyalty to Store and Brand," *Harvard Business Review*, XXXIX (Nov., Dec., 1961), pp. 127-37.

Downs, Anthony. "A Theory of Consumer Efficiency," *Journal of Retailing*, XXXVII (Fall, 1961), pp. 26-31.

Farley, J. A. "Brand Loyalty and the Economics of Information," *Journal of Business*, XXXVIII (October, 1964), pp. 370-81.

Feldman, Sidney P. and Merlin C. Spencer. "The Effect of Personal Influence in the Selection of Consumer Services," ed. Peter D. Bennett, *Marketing and Economic Development*. Chicago: The American Marketing Association, 1965, pp. 440-48.

Ferber, Robert. "Our Changing Consumer Market," *Business Horizons*, I (Spring, 1958), pp. 49-66.

Gillies, James. "The Population Explosion—Its Implications for Business," *California Management Review*, III (Winter, 1961), pp. 53-60.

Gloch, Charles Y. and Nicosia, Francasco M. "Uses of Sociology in Studying Consumption Behavior," *Journal of Marketing*, XXVIII (July, 1964), pp. 51-54.

Gottlieb, Morris J. "Segmentation by Personality Types," *Advancing Marketing Efficiency*, ed. Lynn Stockman. Chicago: American Marketing Association, 1959, pp. 148-58.

Grubb, Edward L. "Consumer Perception of Self Concept: and Its Relation tod Brand Choice of Selected Product Types," *Marketing and Economic Development*, ed. Peter D. Bennett. Chicago: American Marketing Association, 1965, pp. 419-22.

Katona, George and Mueller, Eva. "A Study of Purchase Decisions," *Consumer Behavior, Vol. I, The Dynamics of Consumer Reaction*, ed. Lincoln H. Clark. New York: New York University Press, 1954.

Kenkel, William F. "Decision Making and the Life Cycle-Husband-Wife Interaction in Decision Making and Decision Choices," *Journal of Applied Psychology,* LIV (November, 1961), pp. 255-60.

Klein, L. R. and J. B. Lansing, "Decisions to Purchase Consumer Durable Goods," *Journal of Marketing* XX (October, 1955).

Lansing, John B. and Kish, Leslie. "Family Life Cycle as an Independent Variable," *Marketing and The Behavioral Sciences,* ed. Perry J. Bliss. Boston: Allyn and Bacon, 1963, pp. 138-51.

LeGrand, Bruce and Udell, John G. "Consumer Behavior in the Market Place," *Journal of Marketing,* XL (Fall 1964), pp. 32-47.

Martineau, Pierre. "Social Class and Spending Behavior," *Journal of Marketing,* XXIII (October, 1958), pp. 121-30.

May, Frederick E. "Buying Behavior: Some Research Findings," *Journal of Business,* XXXVIII (October, 1965), pp. 379-96.

McGarry, Edmund D. "The Merchandising Function," *Theory in Marketing.* ed. Reavis Cox, Wroe Alderson and Stanley Shapiro. Homewood, Ill.: Richard D. Irwin, Inc., 1964, pp. 233-47.

Morgan, James. "A Review of Recent Research on Consumer Behavior," *Consumer Behavior: Research on Consumer Reactions.* ed. Lincoln H. Clark. New York: Harper and Brothers, 1958, pp. 93-219.

Myers, James H. "A Competitive Edge in Marketing Communications," *Competition in Marketing,* ed. Taylor W. Melvan and Charles W. Whitle. University of Southern California, 1962, pp. 23-33.

Oxenfeldt, Alfred R. "Consumer Knowledge: Its Measurement and Extent," *Review of Economics and Statistics,* XXXII (November, 1950), pp. 300-14.

Sales Management Survey of Buying Power, *Sales Management,* XCVI (June 10, 1966).

Sharp, Harry and Mott, Paul. "Consumer Decisions in the Metropolitan Family," *Journal of Marketing,* XXI (October, 1956), pp. 149-56.

Smith, Paul E. "Merchandising for the Teen Age Market," *Journal of Retailing,* XXXVII (Summer, 1961), pp. 9-13.

Smith, Wendall R. "Product Differentiation and Market Segmentation as Alternative Marketing Strategies," *Journal of Marketing,* XXI (July, 1956), pp. 3-8.

Staudt, Thomas A. "The Managerial Functions of Marketing," *Managerial Marketing: Prospectives and Viewpoints* ed. William Lazer, and Eugene Kelley. Homewood, Ill.: Richard D. Irwin, Inc., 1962, pp. 386-87.

Star, Shirley A. "Obtaining Household Opinions From Single Respondent," *Public Opinion Quarterly,* XXVII (February, 1953), pp. 386-91.

Stigler, George J. "The Economics of Information," *Journal of Political Economy,* LXIX (June, 1961), pp. 210-23.

_____. "The Economics of Information," *Journal of Political Science,* LXIX (June, 1961), pp. 213-15.

Whiteside, Henry O. "Interacting Roles of the Household Purchasing Agent," *Theory in Marketing,* ed. Reavis Cox, Wroe Alderson and Stanley D. Shapiro. Homewood, Ill.: Richard D. Irwin, Inc., 1964, pp. 270-80.

Whyte, William H., Jr. "The Web of Word of Mouth," *Fortune,* LXII (November, 1954), pp. 140-43; 204-12.

Wolgast, Elizabeth. "Do Husbands or Wives Make the Purchase Decisions?" *Journal of Marketing,* XXIII (October 1958), pp. 151-58.

Wollin, David E. "A Market Profile of the Senior Citizen Group," *Marketing Role in Scientific Management,* ed. Robert L. Clewett. Chicago: American Marketing Association, 1957. pp. 250-61.

"The Working Man, Do Marketers Know Him," *Printers Ink,* CCLXXVII (December 1, 1961), pp. 48-49.

Reports, Monographs, and Unpublished Reports

Atkin, Kenward L. "Communications Patterns and Effect in Super Market Choice." Ph.D. dissertation, Michigan State University, 1961.

Bell, William. "Consumer Innovation: An Investigation of Selected Characteristics of Innovations." DBA dissertation, Michigan State University, 1962.

Carman, James. "The Application of Social Class in Market Segmentation." Berkeley: Institute of Business and Economic Research, University of California, 1965.

Definitions of Terms

Terms employed in the study are listed below and defined so that each may be understood in the proper context.

Brand Loyalty. The extent to which consumers are aware of specific brands and shop at retailers because they carry these brands.

Combined Supplier Selection Pattern. The pattern is composed of four elements:
(1) Information sources used by families in selecting suppliers.
(2) How the husband and wife divide the decision responsibility for selecting suppliers in each purchase category.
(3) The time taken by mobile families to select new suppliers upon completion of a long distance move which brought them into the area under study.
(4) The number of potential suppliers visited before a supplier is selected within a purchase category.

Decision-Making Responsibility. The person or person(s) responsible for selecting family suppliers in each purchase category after a long distance move has been completed.

Favorite Supplier. The supplier from which a family prefers to make purchases of a good or service within a purchase category. The favorite supplier in the case of supermarkets, beauty parlors, and dry cleaners is chosen only after a family has actually purchased a good or service from one or more suppliers.

First Appliance Store. The first store from which a family purchased a major household appliance after arriving in the community.

Second Appliance Store. The second appliance store from which a family purchased a major household appliance after arriving in the community.

First Furniture Store. The first store from which a family purchased a major piece of furniture after arriving in the community.

Second Furniture Store. The second store from which a family purchased a major piece of furniture after arriving in the community.

Information Sources.
   Personal Sources. Information received by face-to-face contact with people—two-way exchange of information.
   Impersonal Sources. Information received by one-way communication-mass media.
   Searching. Information received by personally going in search of data, for example, driving down the street until a food store is located.

Initial Supplier. The supplier from which a family makes the first purchase of a good or service within a product category after arriving in a community.

Intracounty Move. A change of residence within the same county.

Intercounty Move. A change in address which takes a family to another county in the same or in a different state.

Intrastate Move. A change of residence which takes a family from one county to another in the same state.

Interstate Move. A change of residence which takes a family into a new state. This category also includes citizens returning from overseas.

Long Distance Move. For the purpose of the research, a long distance move is one that brings a family into the metropolitan community under study from outside of the three-county area surrounding the metropolitan area.

Mobility. Will pertain to geographical mobility unless otherwise noted.

Mobile. An individual or family having made a permanent change of address.

Mobile Family. A family that completed a long-distance move during the period (April 1, 1966 through July 31, 1966) covered in the research.

Newcomer. A mobile family or individual during the first six months of residence in a new community.

Occupational Categories. The household heads of all families interviewed were placed in categories based upon the family income and the occupational title of the household head. The categories used were obtained from the *1960 Census detailed occupations of the experienced civilian labor force and of the employed by sex for the state: 1960 and 1950—Table 120.*[1]

Potential Suppliers. Supplier of goods or services in certain categories, which the family has not used or identified specifically since moving into the community.

Professional Services. Services secured from a doctor or dentist.

Suppliers. Will include all firms and individuals selling goods and services to the family.

Transferred Store Loyalty. Refers to the loyalty mobile consumers have to a multi-store organization. For example, a family that shopped with chain X in the prior residence would shop in the outlets of chain X in the new community.

1. U. S. Bureau of the Census, *U. S. Census of Population: 1960-Michigan Table 120* (Washington, D. C.: U. S. Government Printing Office, 1963), pp. 24-474, 24-479.

PUBLICATIONS OF THE DIVISION OF RESEARCH

BUREAU OF BUSINESS AND ECONOMIC RESEARCH

MSU Business Studies

ELECTRONICS IN BUSINESS
Gardner M. Jones

ELEMENTARY MATHEMATICS OF LINEAR
PROGRAMMING AND GAME THEORY
Edward G. Bennion

EXPLORATIONS IN RETAILING
Stanley C. Hollander

MARGINAL ASPECTS OF MANAGEMENT PRACTICES
Frederic N. Firestone

HISTORY OF PUBLIC ACCOUNTING IN THE UNITED STATES
James Don Edwards

CONTRIBUTIONS OF FOUR ACCOUNTING PIONEERS
James Don Edwards
Roland F. Salmonson

LIFE INSURANCE COMPANIES IN THE CAPITAL MARKET
Andrew F. Brimmer

BUSINESS CONSULTANTS AND CLIENTS
Stanley C. Hollander

THE AUTOMOTIVE CAREER OF RANSOM E. OLDS
Glenn A. Niemeyer

ELECTRONIC COMPUTATION OF HUMAN DIETS
Victor E. Smith

INTERNATIONAL ENTERPRISE IN A DEVELOPING ECONOMY
Claude McMillan, Jr., Richard F. Gonzalez with Leo G. Erickson

THE ENTERPRISING MAN
Orvis F. Collins, David G. Moore with Darab B. Unwalla

Institute for International Business and Economic Development Studies

MSU International Business and Economic Studies

Michigan's Commerce and Commercial Policy Study
John L. Hazard

International Dimensions in Business
Recent Readings from Business Topics

Management Development and Education in the Soviet Union
Barry M. Richman

The United States Overseas Executive:
His Orientations and Career Patterns
Richard F. Gonzalez and Anant R. Negandhi

Steel and Economic Development: Capital-Output
Ratios in Three Latin American Steel Plants
David G. Greene

Alternative Commercial Policies — Their Effect
on the American Economy
Mordechai E. Kreinin

Institution Building in Business Administration—
The Brazilian Experience
Donald A. Taylor

The Optimal Staging and Phasing of Multi-product Capacity
Harold H. Wein and V. P. Sreedharan

Institute of Public Utilities

MSU Public Utilities Studies

Development of Separations Principles in the
Telephone Industry
Richard Gabel

Performance Under Regulation
Harry M. Trebing, editor

Mid-Continent Area Power Planners
W. Stewart Nelson

Rate of Return Under Regulation:
New Directions and Perspectives
Harry M. Trebing, and R. Hayden Howard, editors

MSU Public Utilities Papers

Selected Structure and Allocation
Problems in the Regulated Industries
Manley R. Irwin and Milton Russell